ADVANCE PRAISE FOR *RECAPTU*

"An excellent introduction to the theological convictions and spiritual emphases of John and Charles Wesley. Paul Chilcote captures faithfully the deep concern of the Wesley brothers to hold together dimensions of Christian faith and practice that are all too often cast in opposition, and he presents it in very accessible form. There is no better starting place for those who have been reminded of the vital contributions of the Wesleys to begin to explore the beliefs and practices that undergirded their ministry."

RANDY L. MADDOX, PAUL T. WALLS PROFESSOR OF
WESLEYAN THEOLOGY, SEATTLE PACIFIC UNIVERSITY

"Paul Chilcote has given us a readable and inspiring introduction to the heart of the Wesleyan vision. His account of the Wesley brothers' 'both/and' approach to theology and practice has direct implications for the contemporary church. This book will not only inform but enable readers to be drawn closer to God and neighbor and to grow in God's love."

HENRY H. KNIGHT III, E. STANLEY JONES PROFESSOR OF
EVANGELISM, SAINT PAUL SCHOOL OF THEOLOGY

"John Wesley and his brother Charles are often portrayed as a kind of footnote in church history, representatives of an overly emotional religion that came along to counterbalance the excesses of dry, Protestant scholasticism. Paul Chilcote blows open this pigeonholing by showing the depth and balance of the Wesleys' theological apprehension of the gospel. This book will help a new generation of Christians appreciate the power and scope of that often underrepresented side of the Christian tradition, where human freedom is taken seriously as God's initiating grace is celebrated."

GREGORY S. CLAPPER, PROFESSOR OF RELIGION AND PHILOSOPHY,
UNIVERSITY OF INDIANAPOLIS, AND LECTURER IN UNITED METHODIST
STUDIES, CHRISTIAN THEOLOGICAL SEMINARY

"*Recapturing the Wesleys' Vision* intentionally focuses on both the truths of Christianity and the life of Christians within the context of the central gospel message of the love of God. This book well develops the Wesleys' grand vision of the Christian life lived within a knowledge of God in Christ, and challenges the believer dynamically and creatively to live out the truths of that knowledge in an active faith. Here is indeed a masterful and compelling book by Paul Chilcote, building on his previous studies of the Wesleyan tradition and basing his writing on the Scriptures and on key Wesleyan texts. This work encourages the reader to embrace the Wesleyan balance of knowledge and vital piety, and makes readily available the joy of doing so."

ROGER J. GREEN, PROFESSOR AND CHAIR OF BIBLICAL AND THEOLOGICAL STUDIES, TERRELLE B. CRUM CHAIR OF HUMANITIES, GORDON COLLEGE

"Paul Chilcote has given us a wonderfully symmetrical introduction to the Wesleys' theology. Anyone interested in discovering or rediscovering the theology that shaped the heart of the movement known as Methodism would benefit greatly from this clearly written, lively and balanced book. Chilcote covers all the essential themes with grace and brevity. *Recapturing the Wesleys' Vision* is not only an excellent reminder of what Wesleyan theology was in the past but a powerful plea for embracing the Wesleys' vision of the Christian faith as a reliable guide into the future."

KENNETH W. BREWER, ASSISTANT PROFESSOR OF RELIGION, SPRING ARBOR UNIVERSITY

"Paul Chilcote provides significant insight into the 'creative tensions' that existed in the theology of John and Charles Wesley, and which often occur in the church of today. The Wesleys skillfully taught and lived a 'both/and' approach rather than an 'either/or' approach to the issues of faith versus works, personal versus social holiness, religion of the heart versus religion of the head, acts of piety versus acts of mercy, and so on. This book brings to life the Wesleyan genius which strikes a balance between these potentially divisive points. Readers will understand why the Wesleyan movement is alive and growing worldwide today!"

GEORGE H. FREEMAN, GENERAL SECRETARY,
WORLD METHODIST COUNCIL

"Paul Chilcote writes a highly readable book that focuses and synthesizes the essence of Wesleyan theology. He presents experiences of the Christian life—including personal and social salvation, a person's inner relationship with God and the rituals of the church, and a renewed heart and outward good works—to demonstrate that they are not opposed to each other but are complementary for a mature faith in Christian community. Sermons of John Wesley and hymns of his brother, Charles, provide examples and grounding for Chilcote's themes. Questions at the end of each chapter make this an excellent individual or small group study resource. Both laypersons and professionals in the church who seek to get to the heart of Wesleyan theology—and their own—will find this book useful."

ROSEMARY KELLER, ACADEMIC DEAN AND PROFESSOR OF
CHURCH HISTORY, UNION THEOLOGICAL SEMINARY

Paul Wesley Chilcote

RECAPTURING
THE
WESLEYS' VISION

An Introduction to the Faith of John and Charles Wesley

IVP Academic

An imprint of InterVarsity Press
Downers Grove, Illinois

InterVarsity Press
P.O. Box 1400, Downers Grove, IL 60515-1426
World Wide Web: www.ivpress.com
E-mail: email@ivpress.com

InterVarsity Press® is the book-publishing division of InterVarsity Christian Fellowship/USA®, a student movement active on campus at hundreds of universities, colleges and schools of nursing in the United States of America, and a member movement of the International Fellowship of Evangelical Students. For information about local and regional activities, write Public Relations Dept., InterVarsity Christian Fellowship/USA, 6400 Schroeder Rd., P.O. Box 7895, Madison, WI 53707-7895, or visit the IVCF website at <www.intervarsity.org>.

Scripture quotations, unless otherwise noted, are from the New Revised Standard Version of the Bible, *copyright 1989 by the Division of Christian Education of the National Council of the Churches of Christ in the USA. Used by permission. All rights reserved.*

Design: Cindy Kiple

Images: Hulton Archive

ISBN 978-0-8308-2743-5

Printed in the United States of America ∞

Library of Congress Cataloging-in-Publication Data

Chilcote, Paul Wesley, 1954-
  Recapturing the Wesleys' vision: an introduction to the faith of
John and Charles Wesley/Paul Wesley Chilcote.
    p. cm.
Includes bibliographical references (p.   ) and index.
  ISBN 0-8308-2743-9 (pbk.)
  1. Wesley, John, 1703-1791. 2. Wesley, Charles, 1707-1788. 3.
Methodist Church—Doctrines. I. Title.
  BX8495.W5C515 2004
  230'.7—dc22

                              2003020595

P 23 22 21 20 19 18 17 16 15 14 13 12 11 10 9 8 7 6 5

Y 23 22 21 20 19 18 17 16 15 14 13 12 11 10 09 08 07

For Frank and Nellie Baker,

Bob Cushman, Donald English

and McMurry Richey

CONTENTS

A Note on the References

Quoted material from *The Bicentennial Edition of the Works of John Wesley* will simply be cited as *Works*.

If the quotation is from a sermon, it will be cited as *Works*, and the number and title of the sermon will follow. If applicable, the paragraph and line number will also be noted. For example, *Works*, Sermon 2, "Sermon on the Mount," 2.6.

If the quotation is from a journal, it will be cited as "*Works*, Journal," and the date of the article will follow. For example, *Works*, Journal, June 3, 1738.

If the quotation is from *A Collection of Hymns for the Use of the People Called Methodists* (1780)—Volume 7 of *The Bicentennial Edition of the Works of John Wesley*—the reference will appear as *Hymns* (1780), and the number of the hymn will also be cited. For example, *Hymns* (1780), 461.

Some quotations come from the Thomas Jackson edition of *The Works of John Wesley*. In such a case, the volume and page number will follow, as in a standard citation. For example, *Works* (Jackson), 14:238.

Any other quoted material will be followed by a shortened reference. Full listings for *The Bicentennial Edition of the Works of John Wesley, The Works of John Wesley* and other references can be found in the bibliography at the end of the book.

PREFACE

My roots are deep in the Wesleyan heritage. Despite my being born into this tradition, however, I have made it my own over the years. It is the "place" in which I have chosen to stay through my journey of faith, having encountered and experimented with other paths. One of my reasons for rooting myself in Wesleyan Christianity is the balance I found in its original form in the eighteenth century. In one way or another, that balance has been renewed through successive generations. But I believe contemporary churches that identify themselves with the Wesleys need to recover something of the dynamism of the early Methodist movement. Even more importantly, Wesleyan theology has an important contribution to make to contemporary Christianity as a whole. It is a "both/and" rather than an "either/or" theology, a bridge-building tradition that can speak with clarity and healing to an age of serious division in God's family.

The first paper I ever wrote on Wesleyan theology during my seminary years I entitled "Both/And." Pretty cryptic, but descriptive of this synthetic or conjunctive discovery. Just before leaving for a period of study in England, on Aldersgate Day, May 24, 1981, I heard Geoffrey Wainwright preach at Rockefeller Memorial Chapel on the campus of the University of Chicago. I will never forget his words about Wesley's understanding of Word and sacrament, faith and works, order and freedom. (I have my notes on the back of the bulletin!) Shortly thereafter, when I taught the history and doctrine of Methodism at Wesley College in Bristol, England, my teaching partner, Donald English, asked me to deal with the "creative tensions" in

John Wesley's theology. That was Donald's way of describing Wesley's ability to hold things together. Through years of teaching these things in Africa, I was always impressed with the way in which Wesley's holism resonated with the African spirit. It seemed to cross cultures readily and contribute creatively to widely differing contexts.

Two books in particular further convinced me that this was a major contribution of the Wesleys to the history of Christian thought. The first was Albert Outler's little classic *Theology in the Wesleyan Spirit*. He described Wesley as a theologian who had mastered the secret art of plastic synthesis, particularly examining one of the most central conjunctions in his theology, namely that of justification by faith (drawn from the Protestant heritage) and sanctification of life (drawn from both the Roman Catholic and Orthodox traditions). Howard Snyder's *The Radical Wesley* further confirmed Wesley's synthetic theological method and its practical application in my own thinking.

Most books on the Wesleys and their theology stress the centrality of their doctrine of salvation. Albert Outler popularized the classical terminology, Wesley's *ordo salutis* (order of salvation), and many studies use this order as a framework for the discussion of Wesleyan theology. If Luther's theology is centered in the *theologia crucis* (theology of the cross), and if Calvin's theology revolves around his conception of the sovereignty of God, then the organizing principle of Wesleyan theology is certainly God's grace as it applies to salvation. I do not disagree with this conclusion. But I do see the Wesleyan conception of salvation as *both* forensic (legal) *and* therapeutic (healing or restoring), as *both* Christ's work for us *and* the Spirit's work in us, as *both* freedom from sin *and* freedom to love. What I propose to share with you here is some sustained reflection on this big picture.

At a recent conference on the future of Wesleyan theology, held in Atlanta and gathering together some of the major voices within the tradition from around the world, it struck me that nearly every other sentence had something to say about the Wesleys' conjunctive theology. This repetition was so prominent, in fact, that it became humorous. "Before long," we joked, "all of us are going to come down with 'conjunctivitis.' " Our conversations were punctuated with statements like "Isn't it amazing how the Wesleys were able to hold this and that together?" "What we need to rediscover is their balance in some particular area." "The joining of one thing to another was the key to their spiritual potency." It is surprising that no effort has been made to pull these discoveries together in a systematic way. This book, therefore, is an attempt to open this world for all of the people called Methodist and other Christians beyond this circle, just as much as it is intended for the professional theologians of the church. It is my fervent hope that it will contribute to the rediscovery of a wholistic gospel, stimulate serious and joyful discipleship and bring healing wherever possible.

This book is dedicated to five special people. Dr. McMurry S. Richey, professor emeritus of Duke Divinity School, was the first to introduce me to the serious study of John Wesley as a theologian. He was a fabulous conversation partner, particularly in our mutual exploration of Wesleyan spirituality. Dr. Robert E. Cushman, former dean of the Divinity School and my theological mentor, alerted me to the many nuances and subtleties of Wesleyan theology, making it an approach to Christian discipleship to be taken seriously. Dr. Donald English, British Methodist leader and perennial Wesleyan evangelist, lived the tradition before my eyes in such a winsome way that he always made me proud to be called a Methodist. Dr. Frank and Nellie Baker, two of the most important students of the Wesleys in the twentieth century, shared their encyclopedic knowledge of the tradition with me in such a way that I would not lose sight of the forest for the trees.

In addition to the five dedicatees, I also offer thanks to my wife, Janet Chilcote, and to Greg Clapper, Steve Harper, ST Kimbrough, Sarah Lancaster, Sondra Matthaei, Howard Snyder, Bob Tuttle, David Lowes Watson and especially Randy Maddox, all of whom read through parts or the entirety of this manuscript. I rejoice in their insights and lament my errors, hopefully here corrected. Special thanks, finally, go to several classes of students who shared this journey through the Wesleyan dimensions of living faith, but particularly to the first seventeen students during the winter term of 1998–1999 at the Methodist Theological School in Ohio. The insights, honesty and gentle correction of these fellow learners shaped this book in many ways. They lived out the meaning of Charles Wesley's timely words:

Unite the pair so long disjoined;
   Knowledge and vital piety;
Learning and holiness combined,
   And truth and love let all men see
In these, when up to thee we give,
Thine, wholly thine, to die and live. (Hymns [1780], 461)

INTRODUCTION

John and Charles Wesley were Christian disciples and theologians of the eighteenth century. They also launched a movement of renewal (known as the Methodist or Evangelical revival) that breathed new life into their beloved Church of England. John (1703–1791), the older brother, expressed his understanding of the Christian faith primarily in sermons and discussions of Scripture. Charles (1707–1788), one of the greatest hymn writers of all time, blended belief and praise to create a unique lyrical theology of God's love. Both were concerned about Christian discipleship—living in Christ through the Spirit with integrity and faithfulness. Whether preached or sung, the spiritual discoveries of the Wesleys and their Methodist followers revitalized the life of the church in their time. Their insights are of potentially equal value for us today. The living faith they rediscovered was both rooted in and oriented toward the love of God. According to the Wesleys, God's love, in its multiple dimensions, is the only proper foundation for discipleship in Christ.

For the Wesleys, theology was never meant to be either boring or irrelevant. The ultimate purpose of theology is transformation. And central to this understanding was their view that everyone is called to be a theologian. As you live out your life daily, you are continually acting out and reflecting upon who you are and to whom you belong. For the Christian, Jesus Christ is the central reference point in that ongoing process, the goal of which is to be changed by God into more loving, more Christlike people. This is theology, and nothing could be more exciting or relevant in our lives. Everyone has a legitimate role to play in this unfolding, transformative process within the community of faith. Theology, if it is approached with this kind of attitude, is both empowering and liberating. Actually, "doing theology" feels more like a wondrous and exciting adventure.

Another aspect of Wesleyan theology made it particularly potent. Instead of setting aspects of the Christian faith over against each other (for example, forcing a choice between personal salvation and social action), the Wesleys tended to see matters of faith from a both/and point of view. Personal salvation, they would argue, must be held together with social action in Christian discipleship. Life in Christ, in other words, must be *both* personal *and* social. This synthetic or conjunctive approach is one of the most relevant aspects of Wesleyan theology for the contemporary church. I describe this approach as synthetic because it attempts to find a third alternative to opposing points of view that often tear people apart. This does not mean that you compromise the truth in order to walk an easier middle ground that is offensive to none; rather, it means holding on to the truth you find on the left hand and on the right. This Wesleyan method can also be called conjunctive (as opposed to disjunctive) because it seeks to join things together, rather than permitting them to be pulled apart. You could think of the familiar words of the wedding ritual—"those whom God has joined together, let no one put asunder"—as a simple statement of the Wesleyan principle.

In the Wesleys' day, this was not a unique approach to doing theology. Indeed, in many ways, the Wesleys were simply being faithful to their Anglican heritage. Because of its unique history, the Church of England, especially since the sixteenth century, has leaned heavily in this both/and direction. It has always viewed itself as a bridge church that has self-consciously held opposing traditions and points of view together by means of a wide embrace. The Wesleys stood squarely in this tradition. But the home in which the brothers were raised certainly played an important role in the development of their theological method as well. While both parents, Samuel and Susanna Wesley, had been raised in the tradition of English Puritanism, they converted back to the established Church of England in their youth. In the Wesley home, therefore, a deep concern for individual conscience and spiritual independence was intentionally and vitally linked with Anglican emphases on communal conformity and historic continuity. The wedding of these two formative traditions in the concrete realities of daily living profoundly influenced the spiritual ethos of the impressionable sons.

But theological conjunctions (the both/and aspects of the Christian faith) can take various forms or be described in different ways. Balance, like beauty, is always in the eye of the beholder. Your perspective on balance has to do with where you stand in the continuum between two polarities, or opposing points of view. While your own perspective is personal, it has also been shaped by the community of faith in which you stand. For example, if you have grown up within a Roman Catholic tradition, it will feel balanced (or right) to celebrate the sacrament of Holy Communion (Mass) every Sunday. If you are Protestant, however, it will feel strange (out of balance) not to experience a sermon of some length each week. So it is important to get outside oneself and one's tradition, to some extent, and look at the biblical witness with regard to issues of balance as well as the long haul of Christian history.

For the Wesleyan Christian, in this dynamic process of knowing and living the faith, Scripture plays a particularly formative role and shapes normative Christianity. The Bible provides the authoritative word for both faith and practice. It is the ultimate guide in matters of balance in the Christian life. But God's self-revelation in Scripture is balanced by tradition and reason and experience. There is a dynamism in our quest for balance that involves all these dimensions. The truth we encounter in the Word (the conjunction lived out in our attempt to be faithful disciples of Christ) is attested to in the received faith tradition, ordered by our God-given ability to think and reflect, and practiced in our ongoing experience of Christ's Spirit in our lives. If Wesleyan theology is conjunctive and dynamic in this way, then it will be important for us to keep multiple images of how we balance life in mind. Some patterns will apply more readily than others to the Wesleyan conjunctions you encounter here. Sometimes more than one model will seem to apply to each particular conjunction. These are discoveries that I hope you will make on your own as you view them all through your own eyes.

One of the most common conjunctions is what I would describe as *complementarity*. Two things are held together, not necessarily because they are opposites, but because they fit together appropriately. Think of salt and pepper. While you probably would not describe the tastes of these seasonings as opposites (as we would sweet and sour), you know they complement each other. The image of the balancing scale is another way to think about conjunctions. Here counterweights (again, not necessarily opposites) maintain the equilibrium of the scales. The primary idea is of holding things in balance. The tightrope walker fits this image as well. Or consider the phrase "distinct but not separate." Oil and vinegar are certainly distinct, but if we are to make a nice salad dressing, they must not remain inseparable. Each is dependent upon the other to bring out its best. Their relationship is one of interdependence. And interestingly enough, sometimes we must shake things up in order to hold them together. You can also think of conjunctions as third alternatives, the sum of two things (namely thesis and antithesis) so as to create a genuine synthesis. In this sense, true opposites or polarities are held together in an effort to discover something new and different. Now the operative concept for a conjunction might be complementarity or balance or interdependence or synthesis or any combination of these images, depending on your point of reference. The most important questions, however, are these: What were the Wesleys attempting to hold together in any of these ways? Why is the conjunction important in Christian discipleship?

Let me whet your interest with a couple of examples of this conjunctive theology. It is helpful to see how the Wesley brothers used conjunctive language and images in their attempt to express their faith. First, several couplets from a hymn by Charles:

Let us join ('tis God commands),
Let us join our hearts and hands;

Still forget the things behind,
Follow Christ in heart and mind;

Plead we thus for faith alone,
Faith which by our works is shown. (Hymns [1780], 507)

Note the connections of hearts and hands, heart and mind, faith and works, in these few lines, all from one hymn. More important, in the life of the church today, all three examples represent polarities that are often torn apart. Next, let us to turn to a quotation from brother John:

> By experience he knows that *social love* (if it mean the love of our neighbour) is absolutely, essentially different from *self-love*, even of the most allowable kind, just as different as the objects at which they point. And yet it is sure that, if they are under due regulations, each will give additional force to the other, 'till they mix together never to be divided. (*Plain Account of Genuine Christianity*, 6.1.6)

There can be no separation of self-love and neighbor-love in the life of the Christian. Genuine love of self that is rooted in God's affirmation—God's prior love—must find expression in love of others. The two must be held together.

In the chapters that follow I will introduce you to eight specific conjunctions in the theology of the Wesleys. These various pairings are set within the larger framework of St. Paul's description of God's love. In his letter to the Ephesians, Paul used the image of the four dimensions to explain the essence of the God revealed to us in Jesus.

> I pray that, according to the riches of his glory, he may grant that you may be strengthened in your inner being with power through his

Spirit, and that Christ may dwell in your hearts through faith, as you
are being rooted and grounded in love. I pray that you may have the
power to comprehend, with all the saints, what is the breadth and
length and height and depth, and to know the love of Christ that surpasses knowledge, so that you may be filled with all the fullness of
God. (Eph 3:16-19)

We will examine two conjunctions, therefore, in each of four major sec-
tions. The overarching theme of each part reflects the particular dimensions of God's love that inform an important facet of Christian discipleship
and theology according to the Wesleys. A brief preface to each part introduces and plays upon a critical New Testament term that is central to the
Wesleyan vision of authentic life in Christ.

Our starting point is the central message (or *kerygma*) rediscovered by
the Wesleys, namely the height of sovereign grace. It is typical to describe
the Wesleyan understanding of the Christian faith as a theology of grace.
The Wesleys proclaimed the free grace of God and consistently preached
about God's inclusive love. We will explore both ideas, respectively, under
the conjunctions of "faith and works" (chapter one) and "Word and Spirit"
(chapter two). These foundational concerns constitute part one.

The New Testament concept of community (or *koinonia*) provides the
organizing principle for part two, which focuses on the depth of caring relationship. Christianity, according to the Wesleys, is not so much a religion
as it is a relationship. Christian discipleship begins with God's offer of relationship to us all, but it is extended by means of fellowship or shared experience within the community of faith. Both "personal and social" (chapter
three) aspects of life in Christ are important. Wesley's disciples were "enthused" because they lived their lives in partnership with one another, discovering the "form and power" of godliness (chapter four) in mutually accountable relationships of love.

The third dimension of length is related to the concept of Christian pilgrimage (part three), understood here as discipline (or *paideia*) that forms,

informs and transforms those who learn from Christ. The real purpose of all discipline is liberation. Unless you practice your musical instrument, you will never be "free" to release the music that is in your soul. Likewise, in the Christian life, instruction that involves both "heart and head" (chapter five) is necessary for your wholistic formation as a child of God. God offers you spiritual nourishment in your journey of faith through "pulpit and table" (Word and sacrament) as guidance in your effort to find your way home (chapter six).

Everything in the Wesleyan portrait of the Christian life points ultimately to servanthood (or *diakonia*) that is rooted in love. You can find yourself only by giving yourself for others. The breadth of compassionate witness is the fruit of discipleship, expressed through mission and service in the life of the church. Part four, therefore, examines the interrelationship of Christ and culture (chapter seven) and the transformational vocation of the church in every age. And when Charles Wesley sang, "To serve the present age, my calling to fulfill" (*Hymns* [1780], 309), he was advocating an incarnational ministry modeled after that of Christ, combining works of "piety and mercy" (chapter eight).

In terms of the big picture, then, these four dimensions and themes reveal the Wesleys' conjunctive view of the church and its mission. Everything begins with the message *(kerygma)* of God's good news in Jesus Christ, the story of his death and resurrection. The experience of the gospel immediately draws us into a community *(koinonia)* where we can learn how to love. In the context of this new family, those who learn of Christ receive the discipline *(paideia)* that is necessary for them to be nourished and grow in their faith. All Christians, however, find their ultimate purpose in servanthood *(diakonia)*. Just as in Jesus' image of the vine and the branches (Jn 15), we are gathered together to learn how to love and are then sent out into the world to share that love with others. Or to use another familiar image, think for a moment about a wheel and the forces that make it spin. The centripetal force, which persistently draws in toward the hub, is joined with an opposing centrifugal force that thrusts out toward the rim. The wheel of the

Christian life turns as we are both centered in Jesus and sent in his name into the world in mission. You need both forces in your discipleship if you are going to live out an abundant life in Christ.

In each of the following chapters, I identify and explain the Wesleyan conjunction under discussion. This reflection revolves around a relevant passage from the Bible, a critical quotation from the writings of John Wesley and a portion of a hymn from the pen of Charles. For your convenience, these focal resources are collected at the close of each chapter, with questions to enable discussion.

It is important for me to close by saying that this study is far from exhaustive. While the conjunctions identified here are certainly central to Wesleyan theology, they are not all-encompassing. I invite you to think of and reflect upon other aspects of the balanced Christian life as well. It is also important to realize that neither of the Wesley brothers was a "systematic theologian." Their theology was formulated in the saddle and in the context of a ministry among common, ordinary people seeking to be faithful disciples of Jesus—it was eminently practical. Imposing a system upon a dynamic theology always runs its dangers, but I am convinced the Wesleyan way has coherence, despite the fact that it was not organized into a system and has not always appeared so neat as presented here. Moreover, I have made every effort to communicate this faith tradition in such a way as to maintain its historical and theological integrity. My primary concern has been to package the Wesleys' distinctive vision so that you will be able to recapture it more easily and live it out more faithfully.

Hopefully, therefore, these chapters will stimulate new insights and lead to fresh discoveries in your journey with Christ. As an influential theologian of the early church, Gregory the Great, once said, "Act upon these things, my friends. Desire to be filled with the presence of the Spirit. Weigh carefully what can come to you in the future as a result of the present." Faith and love, the form and power of godliness, love for God and love of neighbor are yours in Christ.

PART ONE

THE MESSAGE (KERYGMA)

The Height of Sovereign Grace

KERYGMA

PROCLAMATION AND PREACHING

The starting point of living faith — of the quest to find balance in the Christian life — is the central message (or *kerygma*) rediscovered by the Wesleys and countless other Christians through the ages. The important Greek word *kerygma* (the first of four terms that form the framework of this book) is rich with meaning. It can be translated into English as "message," "proclamation" or "preaching." In the New Testament the word *kerygma* has to do with the act of proclaiming the good news about God in Jesus Christ. Because of Jesus, we have a wonderful message to proclaim about God's unconditional love and grace for all people in all places and at all times. Since this is the message that the Wesleys rediscovered in their own time, it is typical to describe their understanding of the Christian faith as a theology of grace.

C. H. Dodd, in a book titled *The Apostolic Preaching*, drew attention to the importance of the *kerygma* in the earliest Christian community. It was as though the church possessed a definite message ("that which it preached" or "proclamation"), the center around which everything else re-volved. That message was quite simple. In the death and resurrection of Jesus Christ we have come to know the love and grace of God as never be-fore. The earliest apostles went out into the world with this proclamation and boldly declared it to any who would listen.

The essential content of this ancient *kerygma* was embedded in the preaching of St. Peter, recorded in the opening chapters of Acts. Peter pro-claimed the dawn of God's inbreaking reign, the self-revelation of God in the life, death and resurrection of Jesus, the exaltation of Christ and the cre-ation of a new community of grace in him through the power of the Holy Spirit, and Peter openly invited all to turn away from the old and embrace new life in Jesus Christ. This was the core of the gospel proclamation.

St. Paul's closing words in his letter to the church at Rome describe this *kerygma* in a powerful way:

> Now to God who is able to strengthen you according to my gospel and the proclamation *[kerygma]* of Jesus Christ, according to the rev-elation of the mystery that was kept secret for long ages but is now dis-closed . . . to the only wise God, through Jesus Christ, to whom be the glory forever! Amen. (Rom 16:25-27)

The Wesleys *proclaimed* the free grace of God and consistently *preached* about God's inclusive love. We will explore both ideas, under the conjunc-tions of "faith and works" and "Word and Spirit."

I

FREE GRACE (PROCLAMATION)
Faith and Works

In Christ Jesus neither circumcision nor uncircumcision

counts for anything; the only thing that counts

is faith working through love.

GALATIANS 5:6

One of the most distinctive characteristics of Wesleyan Christians is their emphasis upon the connection between faith and works. To put it simply, if your faith as a Christian is genuine, then other people will be able to see it lived out in loving ways. Faith in Jesus Christ is not real until it is connected to how you live day to day. This is what living faith is all about.

Formal doctrinal statements of Wesleyan traditions make this clear. In 1972, for example, United Methodist leaders declared that the attempt to hold faith and works together was their most widely cherished doctrinal emphasis. I think it is true to say that no other conjunction you will study in this book has been so consistently maintained as faith and works. It is, perhaps, one of the most basic syntheses because it goes to the heart of the Wesleyan proclamation of the gospel. It is the conjunction most closely linked with the Wesleys' understanding of salvation and what the Christian life is all about. Moreover, the marriage of faith and works is directly related to their conception of grace, God's offer of relationship to each one of us that is free, a gift that is for all people and in all people. The central proclamation of the gospel, in other words, from the Wesleyan point of view, is God's free grace received by <u>faith and worked</u> out in love.

Both John and Charles Wesley proclaimed this dynamic conception of the Christian life explicitly and repeatedly. In his sermon "The Almost Christian," for example, John Wesley made the potent combination of faith and love the defining feature of someone who has become *"altogether* a Christian" (*Works*, Sermon 2, 2.6). Likewise, in one of his many sermons based on Jesus' Sermon of the Mount, he argued, "When we say, 'Believe, and thou shalt be saved,' we do not mean, 'Believe, and thou shalt step from sin to heaven, without any holiness coming between, faith supplying the place of holiness'; but, believe and thou shalt be holy; believe in the Lord Jesus, and thou shalt have peace and power together" (*Works*, Sermon 25, "Sermon on the Mount, 5," 3.9). "Peace and power together." That is a potent way to think about the Christian life. Yet tragically, while that is the kind of life most people yearn for, few seem to experience it.

At an early point in John Wesley's life, in an age no less torn by divisions than our own, he cried out in despair, "O faith working by love, whither art thou fled? Surely the Son of man did once plant thee upon earth. Where then art thou now?" (*Works*, Sermon 109, "The Trouble and Rest of Good Men," 1.3). Indeed, the debate over the supremacy of faith (a central truth rediscovered in classical Protestantism), as distinguished from holiness or good works (a central emphasis in the traditions of Roman Catholicism), consumed much energy in his life. The tendency of many was to argue for either faith or works. The effort to hold "faith alone" and "holy living" together was a delicate balancing act.

In his sermon titled "The Law Established Through Faith, 2," Wesley argued persuasively about the need to hold faith and works together (*Works*, Sermon 35). His case rests on two simple points. First, he argued that the doctrine of salvation by faith is the only proper foundation for the whole of the Christian life, if in fact grace is the key to all of life. In other words, faith is the essential response to God's prior offer of unconditional, loving relationship. But second, he maintained that the purpose of a life reclaimed by faith alone is the restoration of God's image, namely love, in the life of the believer. In other words, holiness of heart and life is the goal toward which the Christian life moves, having been founded on faith. Faith is a means to love's end. Faith working by love and leading to holiness of heart and life is the essence of the gospel proclamation of free grace. Faith without activated love (on the one hand) and works founded upon anything other than God's grace (on the other hand) are equally deficient visions of the Christian life.

Thus Wesley offered this definitive statement:

> The truth lies between both. We are, doubtless, "justified by faith." This is the corner-stone of the whole Christian building. "We are justified without the works of the law" as any previous condition of justification. But they are an immediate fruit of that faith whereby we are justified. So that if good works do not follow our faith, even all inward and outward holiness, it is plain our faith is nothing worth; we are yet in our sins. (2.6)

Here is some pretty thick theological language based on the writings of St. Paul. But the point does not require much explanation. Justification has to do with the restoration of our relationship to God. Faith (as is almost always the case with the Wesleys) simply means trust. Our lives are broken. We need to be healed. But it is impossible for us to heal ourselves. Rather, this process of spiritual healing begins when we put our whole trust in God (faith) and not in our own efforts (works). We cannot work it out ourselves. But once we put our trust in God (that is, once we accept God's unconditional love offered freely to us in Christ), then we begin to love God, others and ourselves. Wonderful fruits (works of love) are the natural consequence of a tree filled with God's life. Faith (the means to our healing) is immediately connected with holiness, love or works (the consequence of a healthy relationship with God).

One of Charles Wesley's hymns on the love feast of early Methodism expresses this synthesis of faith alone and holy living in unmistakable terms. He transformed the words of his brother's sermon into a lyrical act of praise.

Plead we thus for faith alone,
Faith which by our works is shown;
God it is who justifies,
Only faith the grace applies,
Active faith that lives within,
Conquers earth, and hell, and sin,
Sanctifies, and makes us whole,
Forms the Saviour in the soul.

Let us for this faith contend,
Sure salvation is its end;
Heaven already is begun,
Everlasting life is won.
Only let us persevere
Till we see our Lord appear;
Never from the rock remove,
Saved by faith which works by love. (Hymns [1780], 507)

Notice how Charles was careful to affirm the primary place of God in the process of salvation. Salvation is by grace; it is the consequence of God's gracious activity in our lives. But the fact of God's presence in our lives is shown, or made complete, in our works. The only kind of faith worth contending for is a faith that is lived out in love. In fact, this is the essence of heaven, and we anticipate it here in loving relationships with God and others.

Another way of looking at this has enormous consequences for the church today. The Wesleys were able to hold together a "Protestant" understanding of salvation (justification by grace through faith) and a "Roman Catholic" vision of the Christian life that is oriented more toward holy living or perfection in love (sanctification). While the Protestant traditions have always tended to emphasize faith as the means to salvation, the Catholic heritage has stressed love as the goal of life in Christ. The Wesleys wanted to hold this means and this end together. To become a loving person, you must put your trust in Christ (faith is the means to love's end). But faith in Christ is not the goal; to become loving, as Christ is loving, is the purpose of your discipleship (love is the end toward which you move from faith's foundation). Some have claimed that this vision of the Christian life is what makes the Wesleyan tradition unique in the history of the church.

Along these same lines, Albert Outler, one of the greatest students of John Wesley, once described him as an "evangelical-catholic" (*John Wesley*, p. viii). While pessimistic about humanity in its brokenness (Protestant evangelicalism), Wesley was supremely optimistic about the potency of God's grace (Roman Catholicism). What holds these two perspectives together is the Wesleyan conception of God's grace as relationship. Always initiated from God's side, the process of salvation is reconceived as a relational process, the purpose of which is healing and the restoration of wholeness in our lives. Not only did Wesley bridge the gap between evangelical and Catholic; he also opened up the possibility of dialogue with the Eastern Orthodox tradition, which views salvation essentially as the restoration of God's image in our lives and communities. When our lives are rooted in Christ (the foundation of faith), then God's own love becomes real and vital, hallowed by our efforts to live like Christ in every way (the goal of perfect love). This particular linkage between faith and works, between justification and sanctification (to use the more classical theological language), between Christ-crucified-for-us and Christ-victorious-in-us is unique and offers much to the church today.

John Wesley painted a portrait of this therapeutic vision of the Christian life in his sermon "The Scripture Way of Salvation" (*Works*, Sermon 43). He spoke of justification by grace through faith as a *relative* change in our status before God. But he added an equal emphasis on the *real* change that takes place in our hearts, lives and loves as we become new creatures in Christ. Rather than viewing salvation as a static act of God at some point in our past ("once saved, always saved"), he interpreted salvation as a process. It begins with justification (faith) but continues thereafter as the transformed person grows in grace toward entire sanctification (active love in our works) as a "flying goal." To see these polarities held together in a visual way might be helpful.

Table 1. Relationship Between Faith and Works

Faith (Justification)	and	Works (Sanctification)
Foundation	and	Goal
Beginning of faith	and	Fullness of faith
Forgiveness of sin	and	Power to love
Pardon (relative change)	and	New birth (real change)
What God does for us	and	What God does in us
Faith is the means	and	Love is the end
Ephesians 2:8–9	and	James 2:14, 17

All of these terms and images, of course, have to do with a dynamic, relational process of salvation. And within this process, which combines an equal concern for faith and active love (works), are other conjunctions as well. The Wesleys were not only concerned that people should experience forgiveness for the brokenness in their lives; they wanted people to move toward wholeness and healing as well. The goal of spiritual maturity toward which the Christian moves is always characterized by the twin dimensions of holiness of heart (internal) or love of God (a vertical dimension) on the one hand, and holiness of life (external) or love of neighbor (a horizontal dimension) on the other. Noteworthy as well are the tensions between crisis (conversion) and process (growth or nurture), between divine sovereignty/initiative and human freedom/responsibility. The important thing to the Wesleys was that, in this concept of the Christian life, faith leads to love, and to be loving or holy is to be truly happy.

In table 1, the final pairing is actually a juxtaposition of scriptural texts. In their efforts to balance all of these polarities, the Wesleys were really doing nothing less than preserving the theological dialogue between the apostles James and Paul. They embraced the truths they discovered in both sides of this conversation. One could say that faith is worked by love (Paul) and works by love (James). This is not a chicken-and-egg cycle with no beginning and no ending, because in the Wesleyan view God always comes first. We love because God first loved us. But instead of trying to play these two spiritual insights off against each other, the Wesleys held them together. One of John Wesley's favorite biblical texts for his teaching on faith and good works, the linchpin by which he secured the linkage between Paul and James, is Galatians 5:6: "The only thing that counts is faith working [or made effective] through love." Faith and good works are distinct but never separate in the life of the biblical Christian.

It might prove helpful to touch on several conjunctions that are related to or derived from this primary synthesis of faith alone and holy living. There is much food for thought here, for example, about the connection between nature and grace, between creation and redemption. Christians who stress redemption in their theology tend to focus upon human helplessness, depravity and alienation. Those drawn to newly rediscovered "creation theologies," on the opposite end of the spectrum, emphasize human resourcefulness, blessing and beauty. What are the important truths these polarities attempt to claim? And what are the dangers of the half-truths on either side of the divide? What could it mean to sing with Charles, "Father, see this living clod, / This spark of heavenly fire" (*Hymns* [1780], 357)? What does it mean to claim that we are both "ashes to ashes" and the fire of love?

Certainly this conjunction of faith and holiness reminds us to be vigilant in our efforts to hold the cross and the resurrection together, the essence of the early church's *kerygma*. It is easy to view the Christian life simply as a matter of forgiveness of sin, on one side, or of cheap triumphalism—victory without sacrifice—on the other. The gospel message is one of both death and life, both sacrifice and victory, both weakness and power. Freedom from guilt is joined to empowerment for living. Pardon and freedom from the bondage of the past must be necessarily linked to God's promise for our future and the life of joy lived daily into it. There can be no crown without the cross. Neither does the cross take on any meaning for us apart from an empty tomb. All of these various ways of expressing fundamental syntheses can be drawn by implication from the Wesley's insistence upon the dynamic tension of grace and works, or faith and love.

KEY TEXTS

BIBLICAL TEXTS

What good is it, my brothers and sisters, if you say you have faith but do not have works? Can faith save you? . . . So faith by itself, if it has no works, is dead. (Jas 2:14, 17)

In Christ Jesus neither circumcision nor uncircumcision counts for anything; the only thing that counts is faith working through love. (Gal 5:6)

JOHN WESLEY TEXT

The truth lies between both. We are, doubtless, "justified by faith." This is the corner-stone of the whole Christian building. "We are justified without the works of the law" as any previous condition of justification. But they are an immediate fruit of that faith whereby we are justified. So that if good works do not follow our faith, even all inward and outward holiness, it is plain our faith is nothing worth; we are yet in our sins. (*Works*, Sermon 35, "The Law Established Through Faith, 2," 2.6)

CHARLES WESLEY TEXT

Plead we thus for faith alone,
Faith which by our works is shown;
God it is who justifies,
Only faith the grace applies,
Active faith that lives within,
Conquers earth, and hell, and sin,
Sanctifies, and makes us whole,
Forms the Saviour in the soul.
Let us for this faith contend,
Sure salvation is its end;

Heaven already is begun,
Everlasting life is won.
Only let us persevere
Till we see our Lord appear;
Never from the rock remove,
Saved by faith which works by love. (Hymns [1780], 507)

FOR REFLECTION AND DISCUSSION

1. How is your faith being worked out in love in your life?

2. Describe your experience of God's grace in your life.

3. How has the proclamation of Jesus' death and resurrection shaped your life?

4. Draw a tree and fill it with the loving fruit of your faith.

5. Read Charles's hymn again. Define "active faith that lives within" from your own experience.

6. What do you trust most? Is this trust shaping you into a more loving person?

2

INCLUSIVE LOVE (PREACHING)
Word and Spirit

Our message of the gospel came to you not in word only,

but also in power and in the Holy Spirit and with full conviction.

1 THESSALONIANS 1:5

The essential content of the Wesleys' preaching was the inclusive love of God revealed to us in Jesus Christ. Charles summarized their concept of the good news in the familiar lines of his great hymn "Wrestling Jacob":

> 'Tis Love! 'Tis Love! Thou diedst for me;
> I hear thy whisper in my heart.
> The morning breaks, the shadows flee,
> Pure Universal Love thou art:
> To me, to all, thy mercies move—
> Thy nature, and thy name, is LOVE. (Hymns [1780], 136)

This inclusive, unconditional love is made known to us through the Word and the Spirit. Here is another important conjunction. For the Wesleys, the Word (Jesus Christ and the story of God's love in Scripture) is distinct from, but can never be separated from, the Spirit of God.

The Wesleys expressed the inseparability of these "two grand channels of God's grace" in a number of different ways. John instructed his followers, for example, to have one rule (the Word of God) and one guide (the Spirit of Christ), which together would enable them to progress in their faith in childlike simplicity. He also talked about hearing the Word and imbibing the Spirit. That is how Christ conforms our lives to his own image, or as the Wesleys liked to say, "transcribes his life in our own." He uses this expression in his "Preface to the Notes on the New Testament" (*Works* [Jackson], 14:238). "You, whom he ordained to be," Charles sings, "Transcripts of the Trinity" (*Hymns* [1780], 7). In one of his hymns specifically written on the Trinity, he further elevates the work of the Spirit in the life of the believer:

> *Oh that we are now, in love renewed,*
>   *Might blameless in thy sight appear;*
> *Wake we in thy similitude,*
>   *Stamped with the Triune character;*
> *Flesh, spirit, soul, to thee resign,*
>   *And live and die entirely thine!* (Hymns [1780], 253)

In many of his sermons, John described how the Word and Spirit work together to reveal God to us. He defined unbelievers, in fact, as those who are strangers to the work of the Holy Spirit bearing witness to the Word in their hearts. They have no familiarity with God, and the love of God is a foreign concept to them. Over and over again, in the writings of the Wesleys, you encounter the following pointed phrases:

- "His Word came with the demonstration of his Spirit."

- "The Spirit applied the Word to our hearts and our lives."

- "The Holy Spirit enables us to perceive a peculiar light and glory in the Word of God."

- "The Word, applied by the Holy Spirit, shall be a light in all our ways and a lamp unto our path."

Whereas the work of Jesus Christ—the Word—is the foundation of our new life with God (what God does *for* us by grace), the work of the Holy Spirit is the realization of God's love in our lives (what God does *in* us by grace). There is no question that, for the Wesleys, the Word and the Spirit belonged together.

In many respects, the Wesleyan revival was a rediscovery of the Bible. In his preface to *Sermons on Several Occasions,* John wrote:

> I want to know one thing, the way to heaven—how to land safe on that happy shore. God himself has condescended to teach the way: for this very end he came from heaven. He hath written it down in a book. O give me that book! At any price give me the Book of God! I have it. Here is knowledge enough for me. Let me be *homo unius libri* [a man of one book]. (*Works* [Jackson], 5:3)

The Christianity he preached was scriptural Christianity; his understanding of salvation, the scriptural way. Early Methodism was a rediscovery of the Word, meaning both Jesus Christ and the Bible. It should be no surprise to us, therefore, that the primary means of expressing Methodist doctrine were originally discussions of Scripture. Wesley's *Sermons* and his *Notes on the New Testament* are still the standard books of Wesleyan doctrine.

But the Bible and Jesus Christ were not simply objective realities to Wesley; they were living and dynamic. Their vitality sprang from their connectedness with the Spirit of God. If the Bible and Jesus reveal God's love for us, then the Spirit is the instrument of that love—the force, energy and power that make that love real for *me.* At the conclusion of his lengthy "Treatise on Original Sin," Wesley indicated the interconnectedness of the Word and the Spirit: "It is by the word the Spirit teacheth; but unless he teach, all other teaching is to little purpose. You will never see yourself aright, till he light his candle in your breast. Neither the fulness and glory of Christ, nor the corruption or vileness of our nature, ever were, or can be, rightly learned, but where the Spirit of Christ is the teacher" (*Works* [Jackson], 9:464).

One of the most potent phrases to come from the pen of John Wesley is repeated often in his prayers. He prayed for the Word of salvation *sounding* in our ears and the *Spirit* of God *striving* with our hearts.

Whenever Word and Spirit come together as God intends, the conse-

quence is liberation. Where the Spirit of the Lord is, there is freedom—
freedom from sin, freedom to be, to love, to give and to share. And all of it
is according to the written Word. Methodist people witnessed and sang
about this kind of liberation. On one occasion, John recorded in his journal, "The word sunk into their hearts, so that when we met in the evening
they did not seem to be the same persons. They appeared to breathe quite
another spirit" (*Works*, Journal, June 24, 1762). Charles put it to verse:

> *Long my imprisoned spirit lay,*
> *Fast bound in sin and nature's night.*
> *Thine eye diffused a quick'ning ray;*
> *I woke; the dungeon flamed with light.*
> *My chains fell off, my heart was free,*
> *I rose, went forth, and followed thee.* (Hymns [1780], 193)

The "quick'ning ray" was nothing other than the Spirit transforming the
truth of God's love revealed in Christ into something real and present.

In his sermon "On Predestination," John Wesley described this Word-Spirit
synthesis in terms of the inward and outward call of God upon our lives.

> Could you take a view of all those upon earth who are now *sanctified*,
> you would find, not one of these had been sanctified till after he was
> *called*. He was first called, not only with an outward call by the Word
> and the messengers of God, but likewise with an inward call by his
> Spirit applying his Word, enabling him to believe in the only begot-
> ten Son of God, and bearing testimony with his spirit that he was a
> child of God. And it was by this very means they were all sanctified.
> It was by a sense of the love of God shed abroad in his heart that every
> one of them was enabled to love God. Loving God, he loved his
> neighbour as himself, and had power to walk in all his command-
> ments blameless. (*Works*, Sermon 58, §12)

In this passage, Word and Spirit are said to work together to liberate love in
the life of the believer. When we truly encounter the Word—the living

Lord of the Scriptures—and receive the Spirit into our lives, miraculous change takes place.

The interdependence of Word and Spirit is most apparent, perhaps, in the Wesleyan understanding of the Bible. The words of Scripture are the language of simple, everyday life. In that sense there is nothing special about the words themselves. But the words of the Bible bear witness to the Word. And whenever the words of Scripture come together with the Spirit and ourselves, then those words become the living Word for us here and now. That is what is so exciting about living in the Scriptures. John Wesley believed that the Spirit of God not only once inspired those who wrote the Bible, but continually inspires, supernaturally assists, those that read it with earnest prayer. The Bible is like a mirror in which you can see yourself more clearly, if you dare to look. This is where you and I can meet ourselves. This "double inspiration" makes the Bible much more than a recipe book or a static guide to living. It means that the Bible is dynamic and transforming, because the Spirit is both in it and present with us. This is where you and I can truly meet God! So the Spirit informs, forms and transforms me as I read and am read by Scripture.

Charles's verse makes all these points clearly:

> *While now thine oracles we read*
> *With earnest prayer and strong desire,*
> *O let thy Spirit from thee proceed*
> *Our souls to waken and inspire,*
> *Our weakness help, our darkness chase,*
> *And guide us by the light of grace.*
>
> *The secret lessons of thy grace*
> *Transmitted through the Word, repeat,*
> *And train us up in all thy ways*
> *To make us in thy will complete;*
> *Fulfil thy love's redeeming plan,*
> *And bring us to a perfect man.* (Hymns [1780], 87)

In this hymn, which Charles indicated was to be sung before reading the Scriptures, you hear of the awakening, inspiring and guiding influence of the Spirit. But you also come to understand that the sovereign grace of God has been transmitted to you through the Word. If you want to encounter God's grace, you must open the Book. The consequence is that you are freed to become loving in the Spirit and experience wholeness in the abundant life of inclusive love.

In these few pages we have seen how the Word introduces us to the Spirit and how the Spirit opens up the Word. True religion for the Wesleyan Christian is nothing other than worshiping God in spirit and in truth, that is, taking God's Word as a light in all our paths. The implications of this unity of Word and Spirit are many. There is an interesting parallel here with regard to truth and unity. What is the interrelationship of truth (the Bible, the Word) and unity (a gift of the Spirit)? In some ways this tension is strained to the breaking point in our own time between the evangelical Christian (who emphasizes the authority of Scripture and the need for doctrinal purity) and the ecumenical Christian (who emphasizes the need for unity in the life and witness of the Christian community). There is also something profound in this conjunction of Word and Spirit that speaks directly to the person of Jesus Christ. The great creeds of the Christian faith proclaim Jesus Christ to be both fully human and fully divine. What are the dangers in tipping the scales in one direction or the other? Here is another synthesis being tested in our time in the ongoing Jesus-of-history/Christ-of-faith debate.

The two primary dangers in our time, however, are most certainly (1) the worshiping of the Bible, rather than Christ, which tips the scales in the Word direction, and (2) fanatical, mystical, spiritualist forms of the Christian faith that shift the momentum in the opposite Spirit direction. In Wesley's day it was the latter concern that dominated most of his reflection with regard to this tension. A part of his concern was that he was often labeled an "enthusiast" (the eighteenth-century word for religious fanatic) by his opponents and had to defend himself against misunderstandings related to his movement. In fact, he was strongly opposed to enthusiasm, that is, any form of Christianity that emphasized the Spirit apart from the Word. Concerning Madame Guyon, a mystic believed by many to be on the cutting edge of spirituality in her time, he cautioned:

> The grand source of all her mistakes was this, the not being guided by the written word. She did not take the Scripture for the rule of her actions; at most it was but the secondary rule. Inward impressions, which she called inspirations, were her primary rule. The written word was not a lantern to her feet, a light in all her paths. No; she followed another light, the outward light of her confessors, and the inward light of her own spirit. (*Extract of the Life of Madam Guion*, preface, §7)

Likewise, he claimed that a certain Count Marsay was not guided by the Word but by his own imagination (which Marsay considered to be the Spirit) and was therefore a thorough enthusiast. How easy it was then, and is now, to rely on one's own intuition in matters related to the spiritual life. Given that danger, the Wesleys always pointed people back to the Bible as the normative and formative source for the Christian life.

Bibliolatry, or the worship of the Bible, is the prominent danger on the opposite side. Without the Spirit of Christ governing one's approach to the Bible, it can easily become a tyrant. A legalism related to the Scriptures that is individualistic and idiosyncratic can be one of the greatest challenges to the good news about God in Jesus Christ. The key, of course, is allowing the Bible to retain authority over the Christian faith and its practice without allowing it to become authoritarian. The Wesleys guarded against this danger through their Spirit-centered approach to Scripture. Their concern was to allow the living Word to shine through. As Steve Harper has shown, the Wesleys read the Word worshipfully, systematically, comprehensively, purposefully and corporately. They also read Scripture through "the eyes of faith" and in the "guidance of the Holy Spirit" (*Devotional Life*, pp. 28-35). It is important to know why and how we use Scripture in the Christian community. If it is for any purpose other than to become more loving people in Christ, then we need to reexamine our motives and correct the imbalance with a heavy dose of the Spirit of Jesus.

KEY TEXTS

BIBLICAL TEXTS

Our message of the gospel came to you not in word only, but also in power and in the Holy Spirit and with full conviction. (1 Thess 1:5)

My speech and my proclamation were not with plausible words of wisdom, but with a demonstration of the Spirit and of power, so that your faith might rest not on human wisdom but on the power of God. (1 Cor 2:4-5)

JOHN WESLEY TEXT

Could you take a view of all those upon earth who are now sanctified, you would find, not one of these had been sanctified till after he was called. He was first called, not only with an outward call by the Word and the messengers of God, but likewise with an inward call by his Spirit applying his Word, enabling him to believe in the only-begotten Son of God, and bearing testimony with his spirit that he was a child of God. And it was by this very means they were all sanctified. It was by a sense of the love of God shed abroad in his heart that every one of them was enabled to love God. Loving God, he loved his neighbour as himself, and had power to walk in all his commandments blameless. ("On Predestination," §12)

CHARLES WESLEY TEXT

While now thine oracles we read
  With earnest prayer and strong desire,
O let thy Spirit from thee proceed

Our souls to waken and inspire,
  Our weakness help, our darkness chase,
And guide us by the light of grace.

The secret lessons of thy grace
  Transmitted through the Word, repeat,
And train us up in all thy ways
  To make us in thy will complete;
Fulfil thy love's redeeming plan,
And bring us to a perfect man. (Hymns [1780], 87)

FOR REFLECTION AND DISCUSSION

1. Describe an event in which you experienced God's powerful presence in the Word.

2. How do you conceive the authority of Scripture?

3. How do you use the Bible in your own journey of faith?

4. Describe an event of spiritual liberation in your life. How was it connected to God's Word?

5. Charles talked about the "secret lessons" of God's grace. What secrets has the Spirit revealed to you about your life in Jesus?

6. Take some time to "pray the Word." Select a passage from Scripture, invite the Holy Spirit to guide your meditation on it, and make the words of the text your prayer.

PART TWO

THE COMMUNITY (*KOINONIA*)
The Depth of Caring Relationship

KOINONIA

FELLOWSHIP AND PARTNERSHIP

One of the most striking features of early Christianity was the nature of its community (or *koinonia*). The root meaning of this word is "to share things in common." *Koinonia* can also mean "fellowship" or "partnership." Certainly, this was much more than merely a concept in the early church; rather, it was the primary characteristic of the way the followers of Jesus actually lived day by day. The book of Acts describes the way in which the earliest Christians "devoted themselves to the apostles' teaching and fellowship *[koinonia]*, to the breaking of bread and the prayers" (Acts 2:42).

Community is a rich concept being rediscovered in our own time. It reflects the profound intimacy that Jesus shared with his followers and continues to share with us today through the power of the Spirit. We share in Christ and his benefits; we become partakers of God's grace, sharing the good news and living in the promises of Christ. We also share with Christ. Think for a moment about the verbs we use to describe this with-Christ reality. We die with, live with, suffer with, are glorified with, are buried with and are raised with Christ. Nowhere is this intimacy with Christ more fully realized, however, than in our sharing in the sacrament of Holy Communion (note the word) around the table of the Lord.

To this vertical relationship (our sharing *in* and *with* Christ) we must add a horizontal dimension if our concept of communion is to be truly biblical. Community also addresses the way in which we share *together*. We are joined together in partnership with Jesus and one another in common witness to the love of God and service to the world. We live in fellowship with one another; we live out a partnership within a community and with God in the world. We love one another as Christ has loved us. *Koinonia* was so important to the early church that St. Paul used the word to describe the contributions offered by Christians to the poor and needy. Life together was one of the greatest gifts they had to offer.

Community, therefore, is a gracious fellowship in Christ. It expresses the richness of the gift received by creation and humankind from God as well as the partnership of love into which we are called. Connectedness in these dimensions was one of the hallmarks of early Methodism. Christianity, according to the Wesleys, is not so much a religion as it is a relationship. Christian discipleship begins with God's offer of relationship to us all, but it is extended by means of fellowship within the community of faith.

In the two chapters that follow, first we will explore fellowship in the personal and social dimensions of life in Christ. Then we will see how Wesley's disciples were "enthused" because they lived their lives in partnership with one another, discovering the form and power of godliness in mutually accountable relationships of love.

3

SHARED EXPERIENCE (FELLOWSHIP)
Personal and Social

As in one body we have many members, and not all the members

have the same function, so we, who are many, are one body in Christ,

and individually we are members one of another.

ROMANS 12:4-5

Archbishop William Temple, head of the Church of England during World War II, once said that the essence of the Christian religion is an experience of the love of God in Christ changing our hopes and desires. That is something profoundly *personal*. And nothing could be more Wesleyan. The two brothers built a religious revival upon this simple foundation—the personal and transforming experience of the love of God in Christ. The church, they claimed, is comprised of those persons who share this experience. Christians are, by the nature of their faith, drawn into community. That is something essentially *social*.

Wesley's goal, therefore, was to cultivate personal religious experience in the context of supportive fellowship groups. He assumed that God's love was potent enough to transform both individual lives and the life of the world. He held the individual and the community together, concerned equally about the parts as for the whole of God's design. The consequence was that the early Methodist people discovered the freedom of living in the grace of God within the context of a disciplined fellowship, a committed community. Their concept of the Christian life was both profoundly personal and essentially social.

The personal, experiential dimension of the Christian faith is poignantly illustrated in an exchange between John Wesley and the survivor of an attempted suicide, recorded in the *Earnest Appeal to Men of Reason and Religion:*

> "But I hear," added he, "you preach to a great number of people every night and morning. Pray, what would you do with them? Whither would you lead them? What religion do you preach? What is it good for?" I replied, "I do preach to as many as desire to hear, every night and morning. You ask, what I would do with them: I would make them virtuous and happy, easy in themselves, and useful to others. Whither would I lead them? To heaven; to God the Judge, the lover of all, and to Jesus the Mediator of the new covenant. What religion do I preach? The religion of love; the law of kindness brought to light by the gospel. What is this good for? To make all who receive it enjoy God and themselves: To make them like God; lovers of all; contented in their lives; and crying out at their death, in calm assurance, 'O grave, where is thy victory! Thanks be unto God, who giveth me the victory, through my Lord Jesus Christ.' " (§19)

In similar fashion, in his sermon "The Scripture Way of Salvation," he emphasized the personal nature of faith, which is "a divine evidence and conviction, not only that 'God was in Christ, reconciling the world unto himself,' but also that Christ 'loved *me* and gave himself for *me*' " (*Works,* Sermon 43). These examples illustrate one of the defining events in John Wesley's own life, the account of which he recorded in his published journal: "I felt I did trust in Christ, Christ alone for salvation, and an assurance was given me that he had taken away *my* sins, even *mine,* and saved *me* from the law of sin and death" (*Works,* Journal, May 24, 1738). Personal pronouns are underscored throughout!

All Christian faith is autobiographical. If the liberating experience of God in Christ is to be vital, it must always be "enpersonalized." It must be *my* experience and no one else's. If faith is authentic, it will always find expression in the first person singular. It will be something intimate, owned and cherished. And whenever the Christian faith does, in fact, become *my* faith, there lies behind that transformation a story that begs to be told. It is no surprise, therefore, since this view of Christianity stands at the heart of the Wesleyan spirit, that the early Methodists produced many accounts of religious experience. At the center of these accounts is the story of a personal encounter with the free, unmerited love of God in the person of Jesus Christ. To put it simply, you discover that you are truly loved—unconditionally loved. "I am able to truly love myself, as I ought," the heart cries out, "because I know that God has first loved me."

As profound as this personal dimension of faith is, from the Wesleyan perspective, this does not signal the end of the story. Rather, the personal encounter of the individual with God is the starting point of a journey of faith—the beginning of a pilgrimage into that love which will not let you go. It marks the beginning of a loving relationship that draws a person into a whole new set of relationships within the family of God. In *A Plain Account of Genuine Christianity*, John Wesley drew attention to this larger dimension of the discovery. He described the kind of love for others that this newfound love elicits in the believer. Its social dimension becomes clear:

> His love to these, so to all mankind, is in itself generous and disinterested, springing from no view of advantage to himself, from no regard to profit or praise; no, nor even the pleasure of loving. This is the daughter, not the parent, of his affection. By experience he knows that social love (if it mean the love of our neighbour) is absolutely, essentially different from self-love, even of the most allowable kind, just as different as the objects at which they point. And yet it is sure that, if they are under due regulations, each will give additional force to the other, 'till they mix together never to be divided. (6.1.6)

Self-love (the consequence of knowing that God loves and values *me*) must be connected necessarily to social love (loving my neighbor as I love myself) for life to be truly whole. We love because God first loved us; having known God's love, we are freed to love others with a joyful, even reckless, abandon.

For the Christian, therefore, community is necessary, and it is only in the context of a community—a family—that God's love will grow in us. So the Wesleys' vision of the Christian life was one of personal encounter with Christ and shared experience within the household of faith. The Christian life is both personal and social. The great danger in Wesley's age, just as in our own, was the tendency of many to privatize their religious experience, to hold on to the personal as if it were their own to possess. Wesley addressed this imbalance, and his strongest words were spoken against those who would neglect the social dimension of this rediscovered love. In his preface to the *Hymns and Sacred Poems* of 1739, he unleashed his fury:

> "Holy solitaries" is a phrase no more consistent with the gospel than holy adulterers. The gospel of Christ knows of no religion, but social; no holiness but social holiness. "Faith working by love" is the length and breadth and depth and height of Christian perfection. "This commandment have we from Christ, that he who loves God, love his brother also"; and that we manifest our love "by doing good unto all men; especially to them that are of the household of faith." (§5)

Likewise, in defense of his expanding network of Methodist societies, he identified the rediscovery of mutual accountability in fellowship as the critical and distinguishing mark of the movement:

> If it be said . . . "you destroy the Christian fellowship . . . ," I answer, That which never existed, cannot be destroyed. . . . Which of those true Christians had any such fellowship with these? Who watched over them in love? Who marked their growth in grace? Who advised and exhorted them from time to time? Who prayed with them and for them, as they had need? This, and this alone, is Christian fellowship: But, alas! where is it to be found? Look east or west, north or south;

name what parish you please: Is this Christian fellowship there? Rather, are not the bulk of the parishioners a mere rope of sand? What Christian connexion is there between them? What intercourse in spiritual things? What watching over each other's souls? What bearing of one another's burdens? What a mere jest is it then, to talk so gravely of destroying what never was! The real truth is just the reverse of this: We introduce Christian fellowship where it was utterly destroyed. And the fruits of it have been peace, joy, love, and zeal for every good word and work. (A *Plain Account of People Called Methodists*, 1.11)

So critical is this conjunction of the personal and social that John devoted nearly the entirety of one sermon to the point. In the fourth of his thirteen expositions on the Sermon on the Mount, he discussed the danger of viewing Christianity as an "inward religion of the heart" to the neglect of its "severely ethical" orientation. Religion that is purely inward, he claimed, is a subtle device of Satan. Christianity is essentially a social religion, and to turn it into a solitary religion is to destroy it. His argument is relentless. The Christian community cannot survive without fellowship. Meekness is something that must be lived out in our daily lives in relationship with other people. How can one be a peacemaker without any connection to real life, to real people in situations of conflict and struggle? To conceal this religion of love is impossible and contrary to God's design (*Works*, Sermon 24).

In his *Plain Account of Christian Perfection*, Wesley played with the same images and themes:

Men do not light a candle to put it under a bushel; much less does the all-wise God. He does not raise such a monument of his power and love, to hide it from all mankind. Rather, he intends it as a general blessing to those who are simple of heart. He designs thereby, not barely the happiness of that individual person, but the animating and encouraging others to follow after the same blessing. His will is, "that many shall see it" and rejoice, "and put their trust in the Lord." (§19)

The individual is meant to be truly happy, of course; but encouraging blessedness in others is the essence of Christian discipleship and mission. God calls you to let your light shine and to learn how to love in the community of God's family. Social, open, active Christianity—that was the key for the Wesleys.

This, in fact, was the whole purpose of the small groups—the so-called classes and bands—of the early Methodist movement. Initially, classes had a practical function. John Wesley divided the community in Bristol into groups of about twelve members each in order to help pay the debt on the New Room, the first chapel building of the movement. Despite its mundane beginnings, however, Wesley immediately seized upon the design as an opportunity to improve the pastoral care and oversight of his rapidly expanding network of United Societies, as they were called. The classes quickly became the spiritual heartbeat of the movement.

The smaller bands provided an opportunity for intense personal introspection and rigorous mutual confession. A brilliant organizer, Wesley drew up rules for these close-knit cells of from four to seven members—organized for single men, married men, married women and single women—to enhance this intimate, confessional design. Small groups provided a liberating and empowering environment for God's people. Through this means, Methodism created its own leaders from within. By allowing gifted people to assume important positions of leadership within these structures, despite their gender or station in life, Wesley gave expression to the freedom he proclaimed in his preaching. It is not too much to say that early Methodism was essentially a small-group movement of empowered laypeople.

By means of these intimate circles of dedicated men and women, Wesley's followers were encouraged to watch over one another in love. They shared their pilgrimages of faith. They faced the same challenges, temptations and pitfalls, experienced the same joys, strengths and triumphs. To be mutually accountable in the fellowship of the community meant to help each other along the way. Sarah Crosby, one of the most important of the early Methodist women, noted how important these small groups were to her in her journey toward love. "The greatest means of increasing Christian Affection," she explained to Wesley, "is close conversation concerning the work of God on our own souls; speaking without reserve our trials, temptations, comforts and accordingly pleading with God for each other" (*Letters*, p. 18). These people really appreciated the importance of Christian fellowship. They knew that they were not alone. And they sang this faith with conviction and joy.

> HAPPY *the souls who first believed,*
> *To Jesus and each other cleaved,*
> *Join'd by the unction from above,*
> *In mystic fellowship of love!* (Hymns [1780], 16)

Mutual encouragement and genuine care for one another were the hallmarks of the early Methodist people, who sang:

> *Help us to help each other, Lord,*
> *Each other's cross to bear;*
> *Let each his friendly aid afford,*
> *And feel his brother's care.*
>
> *Help us to build each other up,*
> *Our little stock improve;*
> *Increase our faith, confirm our hope,*
> *And perfect us in love.* (The Methodist Hymn-Book, *hymn* 717)

In yet another, and more familiar, hymn from the collection of songs *For the Society, Praying,* Charles envisaged the individual members of a family, inextricably bound together in Christ:

> *Jesu, united by thy grace,*
> *And each to each endeared,*
> *With confidence we seek thy face,*
> *And know our prayer is heard.*

Touched by the loadstone of thy love,
Let all our hearts agree,
And ever towards each other move,
And ever move towards thee.

To thee inseparably joined,
Let all our spirits cleave;
O may we all the loving mind
That was in thee receive! (Hymns [1780], 490)

It is interesting to note that in the only two places where John Wesley put the words *personal* and *social* together, he talked about personal and social *happiness*. And when he used those two words as adjectives, he most consistently spoke of "personal holiness" and "social virtue." His language points toward the realization of God's dream for a person, of faith actively lived out in loving relationships. A Christianity that is both personal and social will always move individuals toward God and toward one another. Not unlike the vision of the fathers and mothers of early Christianity, as our various circles of fellowship move in one motion—slowly and persistently— closer and closer to God, the point at the center, we find ourselves moving closer and closer to each other. And the experience we share in that journey is the experience of love.

KEY TEXTS

Biblical Texts

As in one body we have many members, and not all the members have the same function, so we, who are many, are one body in Christ, and individually we are members one of another. (Rom 12:4-5)

Just as the body is one and has many members, and all the members of the body, though many, are one body, so it is with Christ. . . . Now you are the body of Christ and individually members of it. (1 Cor 12:12, 27)

John Wesley Text

His love to these, so to all mankind, is in itself generous and disinterested, springing from no view of advantage to himself, from no regard to profit or praise; no, nor even the pleasure of loving. This is the daughter, not the parent, of his affection. By experience he knows that social love (if it mean the love of our neighbour) is absolutely, essentially different from self-love, even of the most allowable kind, just as different as the objects at which they point. And yet it is sure that, if they are under due regulations, each will give additional force to the other, 'till they mix together never to be divided. (*A Plain Account of Genuine Christianity*, §6)

Charles Wesley Text

Jesu, united by thy grace,
And each to each endeared,
With confidence we seek thy face,
And know our prayer is heard.

Touched by the loadstone of thy love,
Let all our hearts agree,
And ever towards each other move,
And ever move towards thee.

To thee inseparably joined,
Let all our spirits cleave;
O may we all the loving mind
That was in thee receive! (Hymns [1780], 490)

FOR REFLECTION AND DISCUSSION

1. If you were to conceive of yourself as a part of the body of Christ, what part would you be, and why?

2. How does the "law of love" in Luke 6:27-36 affect your personal and social holiness?

3. Narrate your personal journey of faith.

4. What barriers stand in the way of your love of yourself and others?

5. Where do you stand today in your efforts to balance self-love and social love?

6. Describe an event in which the love you shared with others moved you to love God more fully.

4

ENTHUSED DISCIPLES (PARTNERSHIP)
Form and Power

We have this treasure in clay jars, so that it may be made clear

that this extraordinary power belongs to God and does not come from us.

2 CORINTHIANS 4:7

J ohn Wesley was always reminding people about the importance of both "the form and the power of godliness." In many respects the Wesleyan revival was an effort to recover the power of God's love inside the institution, or the time-honored structures, of the church. Many people at that time opted for either unbridled religious fanaticism (what they called "enthusiasm") or arid formalism in religion. The Methodists rediscovered the power that is unleashed when the Spirit of God is channeled appropriately through structures and means.

It is like the old story about the sailboat. The purpose of a boat with sails, of course, is to skim across the surface of the water. But if there is no wind, the boat lies dead in the water despite the means it has to utilize the wind. Likewise, if the sails are not unfurled, then there is no way to put the wind to constructive use. It simply blows you about—or blows you to pieces.

The Wesleys rediscovered this important spiritual law: the church needs enthused disciples. "Enthused" literally means to be properly filled with God. A disciple is a learner who subjects himself or herself to the authority of a mentor and the structures of learning. And so the community of Christ's people needs to have the Spirit breathing new life into its members, but it also needs to develop structures and forms to channel that power appropriately for the renewal of the church and the life of the world.

It is amazing to note how many times John Wesley preached on the form and power of true religion. In doing so, he was reflecting on a little-known text in 2 Timothy that cautions against "holding to the outward form of godliness but denying its power" (3:5). He often exhorted his followers to "seek after the power, as not to despise the form, of godliness" (*Works*, Journal, September 22, 1743). His experience had taught him that people tend to hold on to the external forms of religion without ever experiencing its power. But he also observed that whenever Christian people begin to neglect the practice or form of religion—in other words, whenever they stop praying or going to church or sharing in fellowship with other Christians—they quickly lose the power as well. He wanted to guard against this at all costs. The point was to hang on to both. And he had ample evidence to remain hopeful. On one occasion when he encountered a group of enthused disciples who "had the power, as well as the form, of godliness," he described them as "panting after the whole image of God." That is a potent image. For the form and power of Christianity, when held together, meant true "fellowship with God, the living power of faith divine" (*Works*, Journal, May 31, 1763). In other words, this is what true Christianity is all about.

Wesley repeated these spiritual laws in his sermons, and despite their various topics and concerns, he frequently returned to this central theme. Consider a couple of excerpts:

> Beware of quenching that blessed hunger and thirst by what the world calls religion—a religion of form, of outside show, which leaves the heart as earthly and sensual as ever. Let nothing satisfy thee but the power of godliness, but a religion that is spirit and life; the dwelling in God and God in thee. ("Sermon on the Mount, 2," 2.6)

It is the more necessary to explain and defend this truth, because there is a danger on the right hand and on the left. If we deny it [the spiritual witness], there is a danger lest our religion degenerate into mere formality; lest, "having a form of godliness," we neglect if not "deny, the power of it." If we allow it, but do not understand what we allow, we are liable to run into all the wildness of enthusiasm. ("The Witness of the Spirit, 2," 1.2)

The dangers on either side are clear: formalism on the structure/external end of the spectrum and fanaticism related to the concern for the spiritual/internal. It is possible for one to have just enough religion so as never to catch it (a spiritual inoculation); it is also possible to have been caught so badly by it that it becomes dangerous and destructive in your life.

In his *Earnest Appeal to Men of Reason and Religion*, John Wesley spoke directly to those who called themselves Christians but were never happy or joyful, because their religion was just a show. He lamented the way they turned a religion of love into a burden, transformed a liberating experience into a superficial formality.

Your formal religion no more makes you happy, than your Neighbour's [trivial] religion does him. O how much have you suffered for want of plain dealing! Can you now bear to hear the naked truth? You have "the form of godliness," but not "the power." You are a mere whited wall. Before the Lord your God, I ask you, "Are you not?" Too sure. For your "inward parts are very wickedness." You love "the creature more than the Creator." You are "a lover of pleasure more than a lover of God." A lover of God? You do not love God at all, no more than you love a stone. You cannot love God: for you love praise. You love the world: therefore the love of the Father is not in you. (§48)

This is a stinging indictment concerning the barrenness of formal religion that had been sapped of its energy and the spirit of love, which was its essence.

Wesley firmly believed that the church is always in need of rediscovering itself, of recapturing its primitive spirit. He even found an important precedent for this early in the history of Christianity. What could rightly be called a Pentecostal revival broke out in the ancient world in the second century. Spearheaded by a charismatic figure by the name of Montanus, this movement, in which the gifts of the Spirit were manifest in dramatic ways, was quickly vilified by many and declared heretical because of its excesses in later years. Wesley's generosity of spirit, as well as his insight with regard to these spiritual dynamics, are transparent in his journal reflections of August 1750 upon these developments:

> I was fully convinced of what I had long suspected: (1) that the Montanists in the second and third centuries were real, scriptural Christians; and (2) that the grand reason why the miraculous gifts were so soon withdrawn was not only that faith and holiness were wellnigh lost, but that dry, formal, orthodox men began even then to ridicule whatever gifts they had not themselves, and to decry them all as either madness or imposture.

In this "heretical" movement, Wesley discerned the power as well as the form of godliness, offering us a model of wide embrace for our own time.

In his sermon "Hypocrisy in Oxford," Wesley argued for the inseparability of the form and power of true Christianity. He carried the argument one step further, describing the interrelationship of these two aspects in genuine Christian praxis:

> Should it be said, "Why, what signifies the form of godliness?" we readily answer, Nothing, if it [be] alone. But the absence of the form signifies much. It infallibly proves the absence of the power. For though the form may be without the power, yet the power cannot be without the form. Outward religion may be where inward is not. But if there is none without [that is, the outward form], there can be none within. (*Works*, Sermon 150, 2.2)

So, in this conjunction of form and power in the Christian life, we can see the importance of holding together the outer practice and the inner self. Each of us needs not only a faith *in which* we can believe (the external, objective aspects of the Christian faith, such as its creeds, its story of Jesus and its forms of worship); we also need a faith *by which* we can believe (the internal, subjective action of the believing self in relation to Jesus). Both must be held together. While the statements we affirm and the stories we tell concerning our faith are important means of our coming to know God, and while we cannot know God apart from them, it is our relationship with God that is the end, or goal, bound to those means. And without that relationship, the rituals, the actions and the affirmations of the mind have little meaning. The point is *both* to know about Jesus *and* to know him personally!

Charles Wesley knew this well and expressed the dynamic connection between the forms and the spirit of vital Christianity in one of three hymns "describing formal religion":

> *Long have I seemed to serve thee, Lord,*
> *With unavailing pain;*
> *Fasted, and prayed, and read thy Word,*
> *And heard it preached—in vain.*

> *Oft did I with th'assembly join,*
> *And near thy altar drew;*
> *A form of godliness was mine—*
> *The power I never knew.*

> *I rested in the outward law,*
> *Nor knew its deep design.*
> *The length and breadth I never saw*
> *And height of love divine.*

> *To please thee thus, at length I see,*
> *Vainly I hoped and strove:*
> *For what are outward things to thee*
> *Unless they spring from love?* (Hymns [1780], 88)

Charles, in his hymn, described the circumstances of someone who has immersed himself or herself in the so-called "means of grace." These classical spiritual disciplines of the Christian faith are the "places" where God has promised to meet us in our lives and nourish us with grace. The problem for people like this ardent seeker is that they easily become fixated on the external means and miss experiencing the internal end, or goal. While the means and the ends must be held together, it is always important to remember that the treasure (the truth, the goal, the relationship) is contained in clay jars (external instruments or means). If you put your whole trust in the fragile jar, you will frequently end up with a shattered mess on your hands (2 Cor 4:7). The power, the treasure, the gift belongs to God, and you cannot possess it. But you can never carry the treasure and power of God's love into the center of your life without utilizing the means God has provided. You can enjoy the flame of a candle (the light and warmth it provides), but you cannot have the flame without the candle. Both are necessary.

John Wesley's sermon "The Means of Grace" deals specifically with this important issue. His line of argument is simple. Christ provided certain outward means in order to offer us his grace. Some began to mistake the means for the end and focused on the outward works rather than the goal of a renewed heart. Because of the abuse of the means of grace, some began to assume that they were dangerous and should not be used. But in spite of the abusers and the despisers, others correctly held inward and outward religion together. Wesley's conclusion is that whoever wants to be in a vital relationship with God must "wait" for God by immersing himself or herself in the means God has provided. We are to wait for and meet God in prayer, in searching the Scriptures and in partaking of the Lord's Supper. To put it on a more intimate level, a relationship grows only if you put yourself into it. The relationship is a gift, but it also requires discipline. If you are going to build a "home," you have to commit yourself to staying around the table in the house.

John said this well in his sermon "The Almost Christian": "He that hath the form of godliness uses also the means of grace; yea, all of them, and at all opportunities. He constantly frequents the house of God" (1.7). And Charles's "Hymns on the Lord's Supper" are filled with allusions to this important connection between the means of grace (the external form) and God's gracious offer of relationship to us (the internal gift). Of all the eucharistic hymns, perhaps none says it better than hymn 54, with its description of the sacrament as the most precious event in which God comes into our lives:

> The prayer, the fast, the word conveys,
> When mix'd with faith, thy life to me;
> In all the channels of thy grace
> I still have fellowship with thee:
> But chiefly here my soul is fed
> With fulness of immortal bread.

The external and the internal, the form and the power, the structure and the Spirit, the means of grace and the grace itself—all these conjunctions point to the simple fact that our life "in Christ" (Paul's frequent phrase) is a partnership with God that combines a living, dynamic relationship with concrete signs of love.

There is another aspect of this synthesis of form and power, of structure and Spirit, that is of critical importance. The early Methodist movement was a network of "societies"; it was neither a "church" nor a "sect." A religious society (unlike the radically objective institutional church or the radically subjective self-authenticating sect) acknowledges the truths proclaimed by the universal church and has no wish to separate from it, but it claims to cultivate an internal life of holiness, which too great an objectivity can neglect. Methodism was a catalyst for renewal, and this conjunction represents the heart of that reforming ethos. The Church of England in the Wesleys' day was an institution in need of repair. It was like a person struggling against the consequences of the hardening of the arteries. It seemed as though there was little life flowing in its veins. During a time of tremendous change, it had become distant from and irrelevant to the world it was called to serve. Its forms and structures had become so inflexible and devoid of life that the weight of its institutionalism was quenching the Spirit, suffocating the life of God's people. It needed healing. It needed a transfusion of God's power and love.

The Wesleys, therefore, sought to be a renewing influence within the body rather than separating from it. They established "little churches within the larger Church." These little churches were the societies. In these catalytic communities—like leaven within a loaf—they attempted to offer an authentic Christian witness within the universal body of Christ, apart from which they believed themselves to be incomplete. They held on to what might seem to be opposites. They affirmed both the necessity of a personal, vital relationship with God, lived out in the intimacy of small groups, and the necessity and validity of the institutional church in its historical form. Their view of the community of faith combined the truths they found in both the institutional and the charismatic understanding of the church. Either was deficient without the other. An emphasis upon order and an appreciation for the past can become lifeless if not celebrated presently in the Spirit; the celebration of the Spirit as the animating force within the life of the church can become divisive and self-serving if not rooted in a timeless heritage of faith. A past-filled-with-gratitude and a present-filled-with-wonder as it looks to the future need to be held together.

Howard Snyder describes the marks of this mediating model (as he calls it) in his biographical study *The Radical Wesley* (pp. 138-42). The characteristics of those movements that have sought to renew the church along these lines include the following:

1. Self-understanding as "little churches inside the church"

2. Use of small-group structures for nurture and growth

3. Structured links with the institutional church

4. Commitment to the unity, vitality and wholeness of the larger church

5. A mission orientation that combines faith with life

6. Consciousness of being a distinct, covenant-based community

7. Provision for and implementation of new forms of ministry and leadership

8. Emphasis on the Spirit and the Word as the basis of authority

This final point carries us back to our discoveries of the previous chapter. All of these marks, together, represent a model of renewal within the life of the church that conjoins structure and Spirit, form and power, in the context of a community based upon our partnership with one another and our partnership with God. For John Wesley, renewal in the church was perennially a "back to the future" experience; it was pouring old wine into new wineskins, fashioning new clay jars for the marvelous treasure of God's eternal love.

KEY TEXTS

BIBLICAL TEXTS

We have this treasure in clay jars, so that it may be made clear that this extraordinary power belongs to God and does not come from us. (2 Cor 4:7)

You must understand this, that in the last days distressing times will come. For people will be . . . holding to the outward form of godliness but denying its power. (2 Tim 3:1-2, 5)

JOHN WESLEY TEXT

Should it be said, "Why, what signifies the form of godliness?" we readily answer, Nothing, if it [be] alone. But the absence of the form signifies much. It infallibly proves the absence of the power. For though the form may be without the power, yet the power cannot be without the form. Outward religion may be where inward is not. But

if there is none without [that is, the outward form], there can be none
within. ("Hypocrisy in Oxford," 2.2)

CHARLES WESLEY TEXT

> Long have I seemed to serve thee, Lord,
>   With unavailing pain;
> Fasted, and prayed, and read thy Word,
>   And heard it preached—in vain.
>
> Oft did I with th'assembly join,
>   And near thy altar drew;
> A form of godliness was mine—
>   The power I never knew.
>
> I rested in the outward law,
>   Nor knew its deep design.
> The length and breadth I never saw
>   And height of love divine.
>
> To please thee thus, at length I see,
>   Vainly I hoped and strove:
> For what are outward things to thee
>   Unless they spring from love? (Hymns [1780], 88)

FOR REFLECTION AND DISCUSSION

1. Consider yourself as an instrument fashioned to play God's song. What
   kind of an instrument are you, and what contribution do you make to the
   song?

2. In what areas of your own life (or that of your church) have you lost the
   power available to you as a child of God?

3. Where have you seen the "power of godliness" alive and well around you?

4. What "means of grace" do you find most helpful in your efforts to be a
   faithful disciple?

5. Does Charles's hymn describe you at some point in your life? What released God's power in your life?

6. God empowers people. How can you best live out a ministry of empowerment with God?

PART THREE

THE DISCIPLINE *(PAIDEIA)*
The Length of Christian Pilgrimage

PAIDEIA

INSTRUCTION AND GUIDANCE

Jesus was a rabbi—a teacher. He used many different methods to communicate his message and mission to those around him. As you can imagine, in the pages of the New Testament, a variety of words have to do with teaching and learning. The Greek word *paideia* is a lesser-known term, but the concept it represents is pervasive. The idea was, in fact, central to the ancient classical mind. It can be translated in a number of different ways, as "instruction," "nurture," "education," "training," "guidance," even "chastisement," but its primary meaning is "discipline." St. Paul placed this concept of formation at the center of his admonition to Christian parents in Ephesians 6:4, where he commanded them to bring up their children "in the discipline and instruction of the Lord."

Much of the instruction we receive is by word of mouth. *Paideia*, however, is instruction through action. Essentially related to character formation, it involves a lifelong process of learning and growth. It implies a journey. Werner Jaeger, in a monumental three-volume study on *paideia*, shows that to the ancient Greeks the concept represented an enormous

ideological task. They were concerned with nothing less than the fundamental shaping of the ideal human being (*Paideia*, passim). For the early
Christian, this form of discipline must have meant something like the use
of action directed toward the moral and spiritual nurture and training of the
followers of Jesus. It entailed all of those things that are done in the community of faith that shape the whole person in the journey toward maturity
in Christ. That is a big idea, a goal referred to explicitly by the writer to the
Hebrews: "We had human parents to discipline us, and we respected them.
. . . But [God] disciplines us for our good, in order that we may share his
holiness" (Heb 12:9-10). This form of discipline is nothing less than seeking
wisdom in community.

While the term *discipline* may fill some with fear because of childhood
associations, the invitation to Christian discipleship is something to be received as a wonderful, grace-filled gift. In the English language, the words
discipline and *disciple*, obviously, come from the same root. A disciple is a
learner. A disciple of Christ is a person who has consented to place himself
or herself under the *paideia* of the Lord, the true purpose of which is liberation. As we have already seen, it's like learning to play the piano—unless
you practice, you will never be "free" to release the music that is in your
soul. *Paideia* in the Christian life involves both "heart" and "head" in
wholistic formation as the children of God. God offers us spiritual nourishment in our journey of faith through "pulpit and table" (Word and sacrament), providing the necessary guidance for us to find our way home.
These are the themes we explore next.

5

HOLISTIC FORMATION (INSTRUCTION)
Heart and Head

The peace of God, which surpasses all understanding,
will guard your hearts and your minds in Christ Jesus.

PHILIPPIANS 4:7

One stanza of a lesser-known Charles Wesley hymn identifies another important area of balance in the early Methodist heritage. Charles invoked the Holy Spirit to bring together the following pairs:

> *Unite the pair so long disjoined,*
>   *Knowledge and vital piety:*
> *Learning and holiness combined,*
>   *And truth and love, let all men see*
> *In those whom up to thee we give,*
>   *Thine, wholly thine, to die and live.* (Hymns [1780], 461)

Here is a whole string of conjunctions: knowledge and piety, learning and holiness, truth and love. The Wesleys were firmly convinced that devotion apart from learning is rootless, that knowledge devoid of piety is bankrupt. The uniting of heart and head in early Methodism was one of the Wesleys' most remarkable achievements.

The Wesley brothers resembled something of a conjunction between themselves. It is overly simplistic, of course, but the stereotype of the two brothers is one of a more cerebral John and a more lyrical Charles. There is little question that Charles tended to "work out of the heart," while John leaned more heavily toward a logical, ordered rationalism. It was a complex balance; what sibling dynamics are not? Both were Oxford trained, but both also possessed an amazing poetic gift inherited from their father. Between these two fascinating brothers there were balances within balances as each sought to find within himself the appropriate complementarity of heart and head and as both personalities played off one another. In short, the brothers were complementary, and there is no question that their complementarity spilled over into the movement under their direction. The early Methodists learned from and appreciated both brothers.

According to the Wesleys, the Christian life is essentially devotion (more precisely, a way of devotion, or *via devotio*). They had both learned this important lesson on their mother's knee in the Epworth rectory. In his *Plain Account of Christian Perfection*, John recalled this important resolution, made at Oxford during his university days:

> I resolved to dedicate all my life to God, all my thoughts and words and actions, being thoroughly convinced there was no medium, but that every part of my life (not some only) must either be a sacrifice to God, or to myself; that is, in effect, to the devil. . . . I determined, through his grace (the absolute necessity of which I was deeply sensible of) to be all-devoted to God. (§2)

Here is total dedication, the offer of one's whole heart to God. In a translation of a hymn written by Antoinette Bourignon, which John and Charles included in the *Hymns and Sacred Poems* collection of 1739, he made the heart connection clear. "Empty my heart of earthly love," he writes, "and for Thyself prepare the place" (*Hymns* [1780], 276). The classics of Christian spirituality also taught John and Charles the importance of total consecration in the love of God and neighbor. In their quest for holiness, the Wesleys rediscovered the classic disciplines of the Spirit.

When they used the words "Christian devotion," they meant a life to be lived more so than a time to be observed. Henri Nouwen said that if we cannot find God in the middle of our work, where our struggles and triumphs are, it doesn't make sense to try to find God in the margins of our lives; the spiritual life is meant to grow in the midst of ministry. No sentiment could better express the spirituality of the Wesleys. This way of devotion is true for your own life, but it is also a fact about your community of faith, the church. It has been said that John Wesley worked until he was half dead and prayed until he was wholly alive. Prayer and classic spiritual disciplines are at the heart of Wesleyan spirituality.

Continued growth in all of life's dimensions was the grand goal toward which all of John Wesley's energies moved. In his sermon "The Wilderness State," he pointed to this essential quality of the life of prayer: "Nothing can be more plain, than that the life of God in the soul does not continue, much less increase, unless we use all opportunities of communion with God, and pouring out our hearts before him. If, therefore, we are negligent of this, . . . life will surely decay" (2.4).

Wesley's life of devotion was disciplined. While clearly focused on the Word of God, it was characterized by an amazing breadth. Wesley drew upon the great classics of both Western and Eastern spirituality. He sank his roots deeply into the best of Christendom's devotional traditions. His *Christian Library*, published in fifty volumes between 1749 and 1755, contained abridgements of such far-ranging devotional writers as apostolic fathers, English Puritans, Anglican high churchmen and Cambridge Platonists; the Scots Henry Scougal, Robert Leighton and Thomas Rutherford; and Roman Catholic mystics Blaise Pascal, François Fénelon, Miguel de Molinos and the Mexican hermit Gregory Lopez.

His personal spirituality, not surprisingly, balanced personal and social dimensions. It was public as well as private, corporate as well as individual. The early Methodists rediscovered the "means of grace" for the Christian community in their day. They saw the necessary connection between the means and the end of vital religion, as we have already seen. By means of prayer, the Word (read, preached and meditated upon), fasting, Christian conference (or fellowship) and the Lord's Supper, God gives and preserves a life of faith and holiness. John and Charles both affirmed this in their own practice and in countless sermons, treatises, letters and hymns.

In his published *Extract of a Letter* to the eminent William Law, who had exerted a profound influence on his spiritual pilgrimage, John Wesley repeated this fundamental principle. "All the externals of religion are in order to the renewal of our soul in righteousness and true holiness. But it is not true that the external way is one and the internal way another. There is but one scriptural way wherein we receive inward grace—through the outward means which God hath appointed" (2.6). Here is the sacramental principle, writ large upon the heart of every Christian.

No richer source of Christian devotion—the literature of the heart—can be found than the hymnody of early Methodism. Ernest Rattenbury once wrote that "a properly arranged devotional manual of selections from Charles Wesley might—and I think would—take a permanent place with Thomas à Kempis, Francis de Sales, and the like, as a devotional manual inferior to none" (J. E. Rattenbury, "The Methodist Prayer Book," *The Methodist Recorder*, n.d.). It was through the hymns—the language of the heart—that the message of God's redemptive love was most powerfully conveyed to the people of Wesley's day. You can hear the often-repeated theme of God's love and its residence in the heart in John Wesley's translation of the Paul Gerhardt hymn:

> *Jesu, thy boundless love to me*
> *   No thought can reach, no tongue declare;*
> *O knit my thankful heart to thee,*
> *   And reign without a rival there!*
> *Thine wholly, thine alone I am;*
> *   Be thou alone my constant flame!*
>
> *O grant that nothing in my soul*
> *   May dwell, but thy pure love alone!*
> *O may thy love possess me whole,*

> *My joy, my treasure, and my crown:*
> *Strange flames far from my heart remove —*
> *My every act, word, thought, be love.* (Hymns [1780], 362)

The theme reappears in his translation of the great hymn by Gerhard Tersteegen:

> *Thou hidden love of God, whose height,*
> *Whose depth unfathomed, no man knows;*
> *I see from far thy beauteous light,*
> *Inly I sigh for thy repose;*
> *My heart is pained, nor can it be*
> *At rest, till it finds rest in thee.* (Hymns [1780], 335)

Few hymns achieve the intensity of Wesley's translation of this Johannes Scheffler hymn:

> *Thee will I love, my strength, my tower,*
> *Thee will I love, my joy, my crown,*
> *Thee will I love with all my power,*
> *In all my works, and thee alone;*
> *Thee will I love, till the pure fire*
> *Fill my whole soul with chaste desire.* (Hymns [1780], 202)

In the third verse, God's divine therapy comes to fruition in the wounded mind now healed and the imprisoned heart now liberated:

> *I thank thee, uncreated Sun,*
> *That thy bright beams on me have shined;*
> *I thank thee, who hast overthrown*
> *My foes, and healed my wounded mind;*
> *I thank thee, whose enliv'ning voice*
> *Bids my freed heart in thee rejoice.*

The Wesleyan debt to the "heart religion" of Continental Pietism is unmistakable. Methodism is deeply rooted in the piety of the heart.

Other influences shaped the ethos of the early Methodist movement as

well. Gordon Rupp was undoubtedly right in describing Wesleyan spirituality as more Catholic than Protestant, being based on love of God rather
than faith in Christ. But even here, for the Wesleys, there is balance. Love
always wants to create the response of love in the beloved. And that is precisely the point. Such a responding love is possible only through the gracious gift of faith in Christ. Mary Fletcher echoed her spiritual mentor and
powerfully expressed this sentiment in a letter to a Methodist society in the
neighborhood of Madeley:

> O that you would therefore do as Jacob did, be earnest with the Lord,
> that his love may fill your heart, as the Scripture expresses it, the love of
> God, shed abroad in your hearts by the Holy Ghost, given unto you. If
> you get your hearts full of the love of God, you will find that is the oil by
> which the lamp of faith we be ever kept burning. . . . Pray, my friends,
> pray much for this love; and remember that word, "He that dwelleth in
> love dwelleth in God, and God in him!" (Mary Tooth, *A Letter to the
> Loving and Beloved People of the Parish of Madeley*, pp. 17-18)

If this is the experience at the center of your heart, then you have to express it. The experience has to be shared. The Wesleys discovered, as many
have today, that the movement of the Spirit is from contemplation to action—from the experience of God's grace to the offer of God's love in
Christ to others. This movement of the "overflowing heart" is beautifully illustrated in a manuscript letter from Sarah Crosby to an aspiring woman
preacher, Betsy Hurrell, in 1774:

> As for myself, my dear, I know not what to say, but that the immeasur-
> able comfort swells my own transported breast! For He reneweth my
> strength as the eagle. I live in a holy astonishment before my God
> while He fills my soul with divine power and the simplicity of a little
> child. Never was I so continually filled, yea, overflowed, with love be-
> fore. Indeed, my Lord shows me the reason was because I hearkened
> too much to the voice which said, Hold thy peace. Keep thy happi-
> ness to thyself. . . . But He now forbids me to hide the light He gives

under a bushel. And the more simply I witness for God, the more does He witness in my heart. (*Letters*, pp. 69-71)

The Wesleys and their followers carefully balanced this form of active, almost burning piety with an emphasis upon the necessity of reasoned religion. John Wesley's great defense of biblical Christianity in his own time, it must be remembered, was his *Appeal to Men of Reason and Religion*. It is interesting how he described the heart and the head together. His descriptive adjectives are telling. He would speak with great esteem, for example, of the person who is characterized by a *clear* head and a *loving* heart. The goal for every Christian, he might well have said, is to have a simple heart and a single mind. Indeed, simplicity is often the key to holding both together. In his sermon "Witness of Our Own Spirit," he defined this spiritual simplicity as "a steady view, a single intention of promoting [God's] glory" that "runs through our whole soul, fills all our heart, and is the constant spring of all our thoughts, desires, and purposes" (§11). Hearts and minds oriented solely toward the glory of God—here is a vision of the Christian faith that must be both caught (heart) and taught (head).

For the Wesleys, therefore, vital piety was essentially linked with sound learning. The poetic lines that head this chapter were written by Charles for the opening of brother John's most famous experiment in education, Kingswood School, near Bristol. Not only were the Wesleys concerned about "warmed hearts"; they were also adamant about excellence in the pursuit of wisdom. John Wesley was a scholar/pastor with few peers. He was as methodical in his study as he was in every other aspect of his life. In his youth he studied the classics on Mondays and Tuesdays. On Wednesday he turned his attention to logic and ethics. Thursday was devoted to the biblical languages, for which he also wrote grammars and study guides. He sharpened his skills in poetry and speaking on Saturday, and he devoted the better part of Sunday to the study of theology. He was one of the best-read men of his day. His advice could easily have been, "Read as much as you can, from the best works you can find, that God may use you as much as he can."

Both of the Wesleys were formidable scholars, and John was a tutor at Oxford. He was gifted with a tremendously agile and inquisitive mind. He was quick to analyze, argue and persuade. He was, in fact, one of the most able Christian apologists (or defenders of the faith) in the so-called Age of Reason, when dynamic, living faith often fell prey to either arid rationalism or unbridled emotionalism. Refusing to separate the head from the heart, his life was characterized by a winsome synthesis of knowledge and piety, intellectual rigor and disciplined zeal. He was, as biographer Henry Rack has described him, a "reasonable enthusiast." He brought the full weight of his intellectual capabilities to bear upon the critical issues of his time. He was an able teacher who had set himself upon a course of lifelong learning. And as Leslie Church once observed, the first Methodists were as eager to learn as John Wesley was to teach (*More About the Early Methodist People*, pp. 1-53).

It is not difficult to find examples of men, women and children who took Wesley's advice concerning sound learning. Hannah Rhodes set out on a rigorous program of reading and study that would put many of us to shame today (see Church, *More About Methodist People*, pp. 50-51). It closely followed Wesley's "Female Course of Study," which he published in the *Arminian Magazine* in 1780. The full title of this curriculum is both humorous and revealing: "Intended for those who have a good understanding and much leisure." I should say so! It demanded five or six hours a day over a term of from three to five years. About a third of the time was to be spent on the Bible, using Wesley's own *Explanatory Notes* as a guide. Wesley recommended thirty-five works in all. They covered subjects from mathematics to poetry and from grammar to metaphysics. The course, he trusted, would provide "knowledge enough for any reasonable Christian."

The Wesleys wanted a well-informed laity who had the skills and wisdom to face the challenges of faith in the marketplace. In an era when women were often prohibited from normal educational opportunities, the Methodist society structure opened doors for the neglected and marginalized to develop their minds for God. John was particularly impressed with the work of a circle of women in London who, at their own initiative, attempted to give concrete expression to Wesley's noble ideals. In 1763 Mary Bosanquet and Sarah Ryan established an orphanage and a school in Mary's home. Hannah Ball, a leading member of the Methodist society in High Wycombe, was the pioneer of Sunday schools in England, long before Robert Raikes (who got the credit) had even conceived of his experiments in Gloucester. She founded her school for the express purpose of teaching Scripture, reading and other elementary subjects to neglected children. She met with the children to provide this education every Sunday and Monday for more than twenty years, transmitting a legacy of sound learning and vital piety to a whole generation of children.

Even more important than these programs of learning within the context of a supportive, devotional environment was the Wesleyan commitment to tackling difficult questions in the pursuit of "faith seeking understanding." It was all a matter of one's attitude toward how we grow and mature as Christian people. In this connection John Wesley was deeply indebted to the great theologians of the early church. Like them, he firmly believed that "faith is enough"; it is the heart that is ultimately central. But he was also firmly convinced that true knowledge enriches a faith rooted in Christ. He could easily say with Clement of Alexandria that transforming faith in Christ leads to the desire for greater knowledge, "and this latter, as it passes on into love, begins at once to establish a mutual friendship between that which knows and that which is known" (*Stromateis*, VII, 10, 57). That is what the Christian life is all about. God wants to engage both your heart and your mind. God longs to enter into a relationship with your whole self, not just one part of who you are. When Charles Wesley wrote his hymn on this important synthesis of the Christian life, he identified the components of this particular conjunction—heart and head—as the two "so long disjoined." It has never been easy to hold mind and heart together. Perhaps that is why Paul prayed for God to guard both "your hearts and your minds in Christ Jesus" (Phil 4:7).

KEY TEXTS

BIBLICAL TEXTS

The peace of God, which surpasses all understanding, will guard your hearts and your minds in Christ Jesus. (Phil 4:7)

You shall love the Lord your God with all your heart, and with all your soul, and with all your mind, and with all your strength. (Mk 12:30)

JOHN WESLEY TEXT

We are then simple of heart when the eye of our mind is singly fixed on God; when in all things we aim at God alone, as our God, our portion, our strength, our happiness, our exceeding great reward, our all in time and eternity. This is simplicity: when a steady view, a single intention of promoting [God's] glory, of doing and suffering his blessed will, runs through our whole soul, fills all our heart, and is the constant spring of all our thoughts, desires, and purposes. ("Witness of Our Own Spirit," §11)

CHARLES WESLEY TEXT

Error and ignorance remove,
    Their blindness both of heart and mind;
Give them the wisdom from above,
    Spotless, and peaceable, and kind;
In knowledge pure their minds renew,
And store with thoughts divinely true.

Unite the pair so long disjoined,
    Knowledge and vital piety:
Learning and holiness combined,
    And truth and love, let all men see
In those whom up to thee we give,
Thine, wholly thine, to die and live. (Hymns [1780], 461)

FOR REFLECTION AND DISCUSSION

1. What does it mean to love the Lord your God with all your heart and all your mind?

2. Are you more a "heart Christian" or a "head Christian"? Do you need to correct an imbalance in your life?

3. What direction does the world around us reflect—a tipping of the scales toward head or toward heart?

4. How does this synthesis of heart and head inform your devotional life? Your worship? Your evangelism?

5. Do you feel that the balancing of heart and head is important for you? For the world?

6. How would the church look different if a greater balance of heart and head were struck?

6

⸙

SPIRITUAL NOURISHMENT (GUIDANCE)
Pulpit and Table

They devoted themselves to the apostles' teaching and fellowship,

to the breaking of bread and the prayers....

Day by day, as they spent much time together in the temple,

they broke bread at home and ate their food with glad and generous hearts.

ACTS 2:42, 46

T he scriptural text that provides the focus for this chapter—Acts 2:42 and 46—describes the earliest Christian community. It was a community on a journey, a people who needed to be guided and fed. The image we are given is that of a family that feasts with glad and generous hearts on the teaching of the apostles (the stories about Jesus) and the thanksgiving meal (the reenacted Passover supper of Jesus with his disciples). Thomas à Kempis, in his devotional classic *The Imitation of Christ*, once confessed, "I am hungry, and I need to be fed at two tables—the table of the word and the table of the sacrament." John Wesley was profoundly influenced by this idea, whether he drew it from Thomas or not. He believed that it was important to hold the pulpit and the table together. All Christians need to feast both upon the Word of God in Scripture, hearing it preached and meditating upon it in prayer, and upon the symbols of God's love in the sacrament of Holy Communion, or the Eucharist ("thanksgiving"). We need a balanced diet of proclamation and participation, sermon and sacrament, pulpit and table.

Most Methodists do not realize that the Wesleyan revival was both evangelical (a rediscovery of the importance of the Word) and eucharistic (a rediscovery of the importance of the sacrament of Holy Communion). The Wesleys and the early Methodists held both together, firmly convinced that both were necessary for proper guidance in the Christian faith and walk. Sacramental grace and evangelical experience were viewed as necessary counterparts of a balanced Christian life. The enthusiasm for the sacrament of the Lord's Supper among the early Methodists was the result of zeal kindled in the hearts of the people by the flaming message of God's love. And so the combination of the pulpit and the table was like a two-edged sword; the conjunction was a potent agent in the spread of the revival.

In the Wesleys' view there could be no suggestion of setting the preaching of the gospel over against the celebration of the sacrament. It was impossible to think about the spoken word (preaching) apart from the Word made visible (Eucharist). Hardly a new discovery in the life of the church, this essential connection of Word and sacrament has been the hallmark of virtually every movement of Christian renewal. It is not a surprise, therefore, to find the frequent mention of Word and sacrament together in the journals of both Wesley brothers. "The Lord gave us, under the word, to know the power of His resurrection," Charles wrote on Easter in 1747, "but in the sacrament he carried us quite above ourselves and all earthly things" (*Journal of Charles Wesley*, April 19, 1747). The Wesleys nourished their little flocks spiritually by both preaching the gospel and celebrating the gospel enacted in the sacrament.

We have already looked at the Word in another context, namely in its relationship to the Spirit (chapter three). But the proclamation of the gospel takes on new meaning as we look at it in a sacramental context. We have already seen how John Wesley recommended that his followers read, hear and meditate upon God's Word. Spirit-led interaction with Scripture was a potent means of grace for the early Methodists. But the rediscovery of Scripture in Wesley's day was just as new and exciting then as it is now. And the fact that the Wesleyan movement was rooted in Scripture is a fact that should never be forgotten. In his sermon "The Means of Grace," Wesley described the centrality of the Word in the Christian life. His argument runs something like this: God richly blesses those who read and meditate upon the Word. Through this means God not only gives but also confirms and increases true wisdom. If you read, study and value the totality of God's Word, you will not wander and perish. Therefore, let all who desire that day of salvation to dawn upon their hearts wait for it in searching the Scriptures (*Works*, Sermon 16). Here is guidance for the pilgrimage of faith.

Early Methodist architecture reflected these concerns. The chapels that John and Charles Wesley built, such as the New Room in Bristol or Wesley's Chapel in City Road, London, were preaching houses, designed to supplement the normal services of the Church of England parish. They provided a steady diet of the Word. Methodist people, hungry for guidance and inspiration in their lives, gathered, sometimes daily, for early-morning Scripture study and preaching that shaped their thoughts and actions throughout the day. The small groups of early Methodism were little more than Bible study and prayer groups, designed to expand the menu of their spiritual nourishment. A vast army of lay, local, itinerating and women preachers arose out of these "Scripture academies." Their rediscovery of the power of the preached word was so explosive that it could not be contained. But the preaching of the early Methodists was balanced as well as potent. Its focus was always on love and love's transforming power.

John Wesley, in particular, was impatient with the preachers of his time who offered less than the fullness of Christ to the masses who yearned for spiritual nourishment. For him, the good news of Jesus Christ was essentially oriented toward God's promise to us—a lesson he learned early in life. "All these days," he wrote as a young priest, "I scarce remember to have opened the Testament, but upon some great and precious promise. And I saw more than ever, that the Gospel is in truth but one great promise, from the beginning of it to the end" (*Works*, Journal, June 3, 1738). Here is a word that brings you joy and builds your life. As John stated in his celebrated "Letter on Preaching Christ," he rejoiced whenever he found his own followers "alive, strong, and vigorous of soul, believing, loving, praising God their Saviour" (§16). This same letter goes on to describe the reason for their vitality: they had discovered God's promise for them.

These had been continually fed with that wholesome food which you could neither relish nor digest. From the beginning they had been taught both the law and the gospel. "God loves you; therefore love and obey him. Christ died for you; therefore die to sin. Christ is risen; therefore rise in the image of God. Christ liveth evermore; therefore live to God, till you live with him in glory." So we preached; and so you believed. This is the scriptural way, the Methodist way, the true way. God grant we may never turn therefrom, to the right hand or to the left. (§16)

Scripture came to life for the common, simple people of the early Methodist movement in large measure because of the way they approached the Bible. They had discovered, with St. Augustine, that the Scriptures are essentially love letters from God. They employed at least three ways of reading these letters, all of which opened the Word to them in fresh and exciting ways. First, just as one would read a letter from a close friend, they picked out the main points. This was an essential aspect of their daily Bible reading and study. Second, they read the whole of the text, slowly. In this way they learned how to read themselves into the larger story of God's salvation. They could see their place within the whole of God's design. And third, they pondered the words and expressions they encountered. We could say (to use a contemporary expression) that they "prayed the Scriptures."

This final point about meditation upon the Word was not something new. It was really nothing more than being glad to spend time with the Lord as a dear friend. It was a personal and intimate appropriation of the biblical story. Their general approach to this more contemplative reading of the text can be summarized in four words: *presence, picture, ponder* and *practice*.

First, they placed themselves in God's presence and asked for God's guidance. Next, they pictured themselves in the story and pondered the meaning of the events and insights in their own lives. Finally, they made sure to put into practice whatever discovery about themselves they had made. Here was the key. The movement of their lives was always from reading, meditation and contemplation to action. They had discovered that love is a verb—something to put into action. And this is why the Lord's Supper was so important to them as well, because it was in the sacrament supremely that they could see God's action for them in Christ. Their immersion in Scripture made the link to the sacrament clear and strong.

For the early Methodists, it was clear that God confirmed the message of good news through the actions of the Eucharist. While the preaching of the Word makes its appeal through the ear, the gospel is experienced in the sacrament by way of other senses (sight, smell, taste and touch) and with new vitality. The Christ who is presented through words in preaching is presented through Holy Communion in action. Wesley realized that true evangelism (God's Word proclaimed) could only be grounded in worship, and the center of Christian worship was the meeting place of pulpit and table. The full, rich and joyous eucharistic life of early Methodism is one of the best-kept secrets of the tradition. It is a tragedy today that so few of Wesley's heirs know about this side of the revival. But one has only to look to Wesley's own practice in this regard—his strong sacramental emphasis, which he undertook at a time when symbolic actions were being displaced in the lives of many Christians by a new emphasis on the mind, thought and words.

The general neglect of the sacrament of Holy Communion in the Church of England during Wesley's day is well documented. In many parishes the sacrament was celebrated only three times a year. This makes the facts concerning the Wesleyan revival all the more astounding. John Wesley communed on an average of once every four days throughout his lifetime. During the great festivals of the Christian year, such as Christmas and Easter, his normal practice was to receive the sacrament daily. There is no question that Holy Communion was the central devotion of the Evangelical revival. You could say that the spirituality of early Methodism was eucharistic. As a result of Wesley's preaching, crowds flocked to receive Communion. The crowds were sometimes so great that extraordinary measures had to be taken to enable them all to participate.

At Leake, one Easter evening, Wesley had eight hundred communicants (*Works*, Journal, March 31, 1782). At Leeds, he recorded, "We were ten clergymen and seven or eight hundred communicants" (*Works*, Journal, May 2, 1779). "Having five clergymen to assist me," he wrote on the day celebrating the end of the American War of Independence, "we administered the Lord's Supper, as was supposed, to sixteen or seventeen hundred persons" (*Works*, Journal, July 29, 1784). At London, on one occasion, he reported that "the number of communicants was so great that I was obliged to consecrate thrice" (*Works*, Journal, November 1, 1787). One of my favorite references is to a Communion service in Haworth, about which William Grimshaw wrote a letter, dated September 19, 1753, "In my church he assisted me in administering the Lord's Supper to as many communicants as sipped away 35 bottles of wine. . . . It was a high day indeed, a Sabbath of Sabbaths" (Frank Baker, *William Grimshaw, 1708-1763*, p. 183). What was it that inspired so many people to put such a high value on the celebration of the sacrament? What had they discovered that was of such critical importance to their journey in the Christian faith?

First, the Wesleys preached that the gospel of Christ is not only immediate (that is, it does not need any particular means to communicate it) but also mediated (that is, it comes to us through certain means that God has ordained). Our life is lived in a world that we see and touch, and we do not need to get away from sense perceptions in order to get to God. The sacrament teaches us that a little common bread can be the means to our meeting God. Just as God entered human history and declared all of life holy through a human being, Jesus of Nazareth, so the same God comes to all the faithful in bread and wine through the power of the Holy Spirit. The principle is clear and important to every one of us: God takes what is ordinary and common and fills it with divine meaning and value. The sacrament declares this reality to us at every table celebration.

Second, not only is the sacrament a means of individual grace; it is also an important social symbol. It is an action that connects us with one another and with God's world. Here we touch again upon an earlier conjunction, that of the personal and the corporate. There are some relationships in life in which we are fractions and not units. We are children of a family and members of a body. As a corporate act, therefore, worship demands rites, hymns, sermons, prayers and sacraments in which the whole body expresses itself and proclaims who and whose it is. And here the Eucharist functions in a special way: it makes the Word that is preached something we can touch, taste and see. The pulpit proclaims a Word of good news to which the people of God are called to respond. But the Eucharist is the act of the whole church—a corporate declaration of the gospel word to all people.

A final, important point at the heart of the Wesleyan concept of the sacrament is this: the Lord's Supper always faithfully proclaims the Word. As Paul once said, it "proclaim[s] the Lord's death until he comes" (1 Cor 11:26). But it also proclaims the new life that is available to all who will receive it. The human witness may fail. In fact, preaching has frequently failed, as important and vital as it is. But as long as the Lord's Supper is celebrated, there will always be a visible sign of God's love and grace in the midst of our brokenness. The sacrament offers Christ in his fullness to us all. Here is a profound relational conception of the eucharistic meal that is grounded in evangelical experience and consummated in the offer of new and abundant life in Christ through the power of the Holy Spirit. Early Methodists flocked to the sacrament of Holy Communion because there they met God in the person of Jesus Christ. That is where they encountered God's love. That is where they celebrated the presence of a living Lord. That is where they received spiritual nourishment to continue their journey home.

The Wesleys had only to look to their mother, Susanna, for evidence of this presence, love and invitation to new life in the sacrament. At a time of deep distress in her life, she informed John of an amazing breakthrough, which he recorded in his journal: "While my son Hall was pronouncing these words, in delivering the cup to me, 'The blood of our Lord Jesus Christ, which was given for thee!' the words struck through my heart, and I knew that God, for Christ's sake, had forgiven me all my sins" (*Works*, Journal, September 3, 1739).

John recorded a similar and typical event later that same month. "[Mrs. Crouch] had long earnestly desired to receive the Holy Communion," he wrote, "having an unaccountably strong persuasion that God would manifest himself to her therein. . . . And 'he was made known unto her in the breaking of bread.' In that moment she felt her load removed; she knew she was accepted in the Beloved" (*Works*, Journal, September 20, 1739). The Wesleys firmly believed that the sacrament was not only a means of "confirming" grace (that is, sustaining the believer in transit home) but was also a "converting" ordinance (that is, a place at which the gift of faith in Christ is initially bestowed). And conversion was the experience of many who perceived the good news of God's love through sacramental actions. To put it simply, Holy Communion was, for many, the most potent "altar call" of all. The Communion rail was a place of transforming encounter with God.

John Wesley, in fact, described the sacrament as the "grand channel" of God's redemptive love in action. In typical poetic fashion, Charles described it as God's "richest legacy" to the human family:

> *Fasting he doth, and hearing bless,*
>   *And prayer can much avail,*
> *Good vessels all to draw the grace*
>   *Out of salvation's well.*
>
> *But none, like this mysterious rite*
>   *Which dying mercy gave,*
> *Can draw forth all his promised might*
>   *And all his will to save.*

> This is the richest legacy
>   Thou hast on man bestow'd:
> Here chiefly, Lord, we feed on thee,
>   And drink thy precious blood. (Hymns on the Lord's Supper
> [1745], 42)

That is the whole point. It is here that we are fed. It is at the table that we receive the nourishment we need, as a family, to continue in our journey. And so the table is a place of feasting and celebration, a place to enjoy God and the company of the faithful.

I will never forget one Sunday morning when I celebrated Holy Communion with my own congregation. A little boy came forward to receive the elements. As I placed the bread into his hands, he looked into my eyes with a broad smile on his face. He was anticipating something great. And when I offered him the cup, he drank with excitement, expectant, enjoying the wonder of the moment. After the dismissal, with a look of satisfaction on his face, he turned to take his seat and said in a loud voice, "Ah! Now I am full." No one had to explain to him that this was a meal that was spiritually filling. He had received a gift, and he knew it. God had filled his life again with love and joy and a wonderful sense of belonging in the family of God. This is precisely what the early Methodists, with the Wesleys, had rediscovered in their own day.

The Wesleys corrected the imbalance between the preached Word and the neglected sacrament. Their conception of Christian worship was one that united these two great means of grace in the life of the community of faith. Eucharist was central to them, not so much because it was appealing, but because they believed that Jesus truly gave himself to us in this act of love. Preaching was central to them, not so much because it was the only effective means of communicating the gospel, but because it proclaimed good news that simply had to be shared. Whenever words are combined with actions, people listen and people come. The fullest expression of the Christian community at worship must surely combine the two; the pulpit and the table, when held together, are powerful tools for love. To come back to the image of the two tables, at the first table we enjoy and feast on the Word of God. We read and hear the Scriptures, not for academic study, but to receive God's strength and love through them. At the second table we feast together on the holy bread and wine. A table is set before us. We each take our place around that table, with thanksgiving, and receive from God exactly what we need to carry on.

KEY TEXTS

BIBLICAL TEXTS

They devoted themselves to the apostles' teaching and fellowship, to the breaking of bread and the prayers. . . . Day by day, as they spent much time together in the temple, they broke bread at home and ate their food with glad and generous hearts. (Acts 2:42, 46)

Beginning with Moses and all the prophets, [Jesus] interpreted to them the things about himself in all the scriptures. . . . When he was at the table with them, he took bread, blessed and broke it, and gave it to them. Then their eyes were opened, and they recognized him. (Lk 24:27, 30-31)

JOHN WESLEY TEXTS

All these days I scarce remember to have opened the Testament, but upon some great and precious promise. And I saw more than ever, that the Gospel is in truth but one great promise, from the beginning of it to the end. (*Works*, Journal, June 4, 1738)

[Mrs. Crouch] had long earnestly desired to receive the Holy Communion, having an unaccountably strong persuasion that God would manifest himself to her therein. . . . And "he was made known unto her in the breaking of bread." In that moment she felt her load removed; she knew she was accepted in the Beloved. (*Works*, Journal, September 20, 1739)

CHARLES WESLEY TEXT

> *Fasting he doth, and hearing bless,*
> *And prayer can much avail,*
> *Good vessels all to draw the grace*
> *Out of salvation's well.*
>
> *But none, like this mysterious rite*
> *Which dying mercy gave,*
> *Can draw forth all his promised might*
> *And all his will to save.*
>
> *This is the richest legacy*
> *Thou hast on man bestow'd:*
> *Here chiefly, Lord, we feed on thee,*
> *And drink thy precious blood.* (Hymns on the Lord's Supper
> [1745], 42)

FOR REFLECTION AND DISCUSSION

1. Reflect upon how you have been guided in your Christian life through both the Word and the sacrament.

2. In terms of these issues, what is your present diet like?

3. In your "love letter from God," what is God writing to you?

4. Take time to "feed on the Word" through the fourfold process of "presence," "picture," "ponder" and "practice."

5. Describe your most memorable experience of the Lord's Supper.

6. Close your eyes and visualize yourself drawing grace out of salvation's well, and reflect on what God has revealed to you.

PART FOUR

THE SERVANTHOOD
(DIAKONIA)
The Breadth of Compassionate Witness

DIAKONIA

MISSION AND SERVICE

Luke's Gospel records Jesus' paradoxical lesson that greatness in the community of his disciples is to be measured in terms of willingness to serve: "The greatest among you must become like the youngest, and the leader like one who serves. For who is greater, the one who is at the table or the one who serves? Is it not the one at the table? But I am among you as one who serves" (Lk 22:26-27). Elsewhere we are reminded that Jesus "came not to be served but to serve" (Mk 10:45). Jesus left no doubt that he was the chief of all servants. The critical word to which these quotations point is the word *diakonia*, which means "service," "ministry," "mission" or "labor for others."

In its narrowest sense, *diakonia* meant "to wait on a table" or "to serve a dinner." Having shared so many meals with those he loved, Jesus naturally developed one of his most powerful images related to ministry from this common and ordinary round of life. If Christian ministry derives its essential nature from the person and work of Christ, then there could be no more consistent theme than that of servanthood. The hallmark of Jesus' life was the way in which he cared for the needs of people around him and demonstrated compassionate love toward all. In the upper room he performed one of the most poignant signs of his mission as he took a towel and a basin of water and washed the feet of his followers (Jn 13). He acted out what it means to be in ministry in his name.

It is important to note (though it is perhaps obvious) that in the ancient world the work of the slave was involuntary. What distinguished the work of a slave from that of the worker engaged in *diakonia* was the worker's voluntary commitment to someone else. Nowhere was the importance and urgency of this personal investment and human solidarity more dramatically communicated than in Jesus' words concerning the judgment of the nations in Matthew 25. Those who failed in service to others, who neglected *diakonia*, answer the judge with a question: "Lord, when was it that we saw you hungry or thirsty or a stranger or naked or sick or in prison, and did not take care of you?" And the response is "Just as you did not do it to one of the least of these, you did not do it to me" (Mt 25:44-45).

Compassionate witness is the fruit of discipleship, expressed through mission and service in the life of the church. Nothing is of greater importance in the Christian life than the desire "to serve for the sake of those who are to inherit salvation" (Heb 1:14). In the chapters that follow, we will explore this transformational vocation that connects our Christian witness to our context ("Christ and culture") and examine the larger meaning of Charles Wesley's words "to serve the present age, my calling to fulfill." Finally, we will explore the nature of an incarnational ministry—of service in the way of Jesus—that combines works of piety and works of mercy.

7

TRANSFORMATIONAL VOCATION (MISSION)
Christ and Culture

The Lord has commanded us, saying,

"I have set you to be a light for the Gentiles,

so that you may bring salvation to the ends of the earth."

ACTS 13:47

The familiar words from Charles Wesley's *Hymns* declare an important principle:

> *A charge to keep I have,*
> *A God to glorify,*
> *A never-dying soul to save,*
> *And fit it for the sky;*
> *To serve the present age,*
> *My calling to fulfil;*
> *O may it all my powers engage*
> *To do my Master's will. (Hymns [1780], 309)*

They remind us that God has chosen us to be servants. God has not chosen us for privilege. We are called to be servants, and the field of our service is God's world. Our charge—our duty and responsibility as Christians—is to serve the present age. And we are to use all of our gifts, all of our powers, to declare the amazing love of God to all. The context of our ministry, therefore, is wherever we live. If this is the true nature of our calling as disciples of Christ, then there must be a vital connection between Christians and the context in which they live out their faith. In order to bear witness to the good news of Jesus Christ, the gospel and the culture must be related to one another in a dynamic way.

The cultural and ecclesial context in which the Wesleys lived helped them to clarify their own conception of the church. They came to believe that there was a necessary connection in the life of the Christian community between evangelism and mission. It is not too much to say that all three concepts taken together—church, evangelism and mission—defined early Methodism. And so the Wesleys pressed the question, what is the essential calling of the church? Their conclusion was that the central purpose of the church is mission—God's mission. The church is not called to live for itself but to live for others. It is called, like Christ, to give itself for the life of the world. It is not so much that the church has a mission or ministries; rather, the church *is* mission. As the prophet Isaiah reminded the people of God centuries before:

> It is too light a thing that you should be my servant
>   to raise up the tribes of Jacob
>   and to restore the survivors of Israel;
> I will give you as a light to the nations,
>   that my salvation may reach to the end of the earth. (49:6)

The church of Wesley's England had exchanged its true vocation—mission—for maintenance. (This is a confusion that slips into the life of the church in every age.) It had become distant from and irrelevant to the world it was called to serve. It needed desperately to reclaim its true identity as God's agent of love in the world. The Wesleys firmly believed that God was raising up the Methodists for the task of resuscitating a missional church.

This vision, as you might expect, was deeply rooted in Scripture. When John Wesley adapted the Puritan Covenant Renewal Service for use in his own communities, he linked this experience with one of Jesus' most poignant images for the church, namely the vine and branches of John 15. In this passage Jesus presents a picture of the church. As we abide in Christ (the true vine), we take our nourishment from him as the source of all life. We are constantly drawn into the center, to the core, to the source. There is something similar here to the centripetal force of the wheel, something that persistently draws us closer to Christ and closer to one another. But the purpose of the vine is not simply to be drawn in, to revel in our connectedness and fellowship. The vine does not exist for its own benefit but for the benefit of others through its fruit. What continues to give us vitality in the church is the centrifugal force that spins us out into the world with the fruit of the Spirit. As we share this fruit with others, they are enabled to taste and see that God is good. A church that is turned in on itself will surely die. But a church that is intentional about its primary mission, a church that is spun out in loving service into the world, rediscovers itself day by day. The church is constituted by a shared experience of the good news of Jesus Christ around which community is built and out of which service extends. This is a Wesleyan definition of the church, and the Methodist people reclaimed this mission-church model in their own time.

It is all so simple. Christ calls us to become disciples (learners) and gathers us into a pilgrim community in order to teach us how to love. Then he makes us apostles (sent-out ones) to serve the present age by sharing that love with others. We are called, not because of what we have done, but because we are God's own people, formed by God's purpose and grace. The true vocation of every believer, therefore, and of the church as the whole people of God, is a summons to enter a particular, revolutionary path of self-sacrificing love for the world. To be the church, from a Wesleyan point of view, is to accept Jesus' invitation to participate in a new age of peace with justice founded upon the reckless abandonment of power and self. In this vision of the church, evangelism and mission are inseparable but distinct. "Offering Christ," to use Wesley's own terminology, involves both word and deed, both proclamation and action; it connects the gospel to the world.

It is here that the sacrament of baptism becomes a powerful symbol of God's presence and purpose in and for the church. From a Wesleyan perspective, everything I have said in the preceding paragraph is a statement about baptism. Many contemporary followers of the Wesleys bemoan the fact that neither John nor Charles gave us as clear an explanation of baptism as they would have wished. Their silence on this point can be explained in part by the fact that, for these two working within the Church of England, baptism was a given and called for little comment. Contentious questions raised about baptism today tend not to be the questions of that time. Lack of clarity, however, has led to confusion on many levels concerning the sacrament, and even to the view that John Wesley's thinking on this matter was muddled. The primary division in the church today has emerged around whether our status as Christians is defined by infant baptism or adult conversion. Certainly, here is an issue that goes beyond Methodism. Baptismal regeneration and a subsequent new birth (conversion) are set over against each other in an either-or way of thinking that is foreign to the Wesleys. This issue is addressed most appropriately in the context of mission and evangelism—in other words, the purpose of the church—and that is why it merits some brief comment here.

Several things are clear in John Wesley's thought about the sacrament of baptism. First, he refused to accept a reductionism that makes baptism a purely symbolic act. Second, baptism is initiatory. Its proper function is to begin a life in faith and holiness, and that is why it need be done only once. Third, the sacrament is the ordinary means to salvation within the community of faith. It is the normal way to "make a Christian." Fourth, baptism is a means to the goal of realizing genuine, living faith and holiness in a person's life. The means cannot be separated from the end, but it is the end or goal upon which Wesley always focused his attention. Fifth, all grace may be lost, but while possible, this loss is not inevitable. The Wesleys' keen observation of Christian living taught them, however, that an experience of conversion (new birth) subsequent to baptism was necessary in the lives of most, if not all, people. But such life-changing experiences did not negate the act of infant baptism. Neither did they empty baptism of its meaning. Rather, subsequent new birth, for John Wesley, was the culmination of the work of the Spirit begun in baptism. In other words, if the question is "Does a person experience new birth in baptism or in subsequent conversion?" Wesley's response would be a resounding "Yes!" We are struck yet again with a powerful both/and way of thinking that has been lost among many in our own time.

Perhaps even more importantly (and even though Wesley himself never used this kind of language), it is consistent with his thinking to describe baptism as *ordination*. While some are called to ordained ministry, and rightfully so, baptism represents the call of every follower of Jesus into a unique ministry in the world. Moreover, it unites us in a common mission to proclaim and live the way of Jesus. As Ron Anderson has observed, the sacrament is a sign of love that confirms "a commitment to ongoing growth, conversion, and transformation into the fullness of the image of Christ in the midst of a community of faith, regardless of the age at which a person receives baptism" (Keith Beasley-Toplitte, ed., *Upper Room Dictionary*, p. 31). All baptism is infant baptism. Regardless of our age, are we not all perennially infants in relation to God? All baptism is adult baptism. Even if it is a baby who is receiving baptism, are not the whole people of God surrounding that child with their trust in Jesus and striving to grow into holiness of heart and life? It takes a community of faith to make a Christian. The point here is that baptism is intimately connected to our mission as the people of God, despite the fact that few people ever think about it in this light. To use the image of Charles Wesley, to be "plunged into the depths of God" in baptism, (*Hymns* [1780], 363, 465) means that we are called and empowered to immerse ourselves in the life of God's world as ambassadors of shalom. And the first great task of our mission is to proclaim the gospel.

There can be no question that the Wesleys defined evangelism primarily in terms of preaching. "I do indeed live," John once confessed to his journal, "by preaching" (*Works*, Journal, July 28, 1757). He considered evangelistic preaching to be the primary means by which people were drawn to

Christ and into the fellowship of the church, where they could be nurtured in faith and empowered to live holy lives. While his published sermons are really more like theological essays for the purpose of teaching, his extemporaneous preaching was characterized by the urgency of an invitation. Eyewitness accounts of these events stress the word "now" time and time again. Wesley's persistent theme was "Now is the day of salvation." In the *Conference Minutes of 1744*, he asked the question "What is the best method of preaching?" His fourfold response was simple and clear: "(1) to invite, (2) to convince, (3) to offer Christ, (4) to build up, and to do this (in some measure) in every sermon." As we have already seen, the central message was that of universal love to all made known to us in Jesus Christ.

He also established rules for his growing cadre of lay preachers, known as "helpers," and the most important rule of all was this:

> You have nothing to do but to save souls. Therefore spend and be spent in this work. And go always, not only to those that want you, but to those that want you most.

> Observe: It is not your business to preach so many times, and to take care of this or that society; but to save as many souls as you can; to bring as many sinners as you possibly can to repentance and with all your power to build them up in that holiness without which they cannot see the Lord. (*Works* [Jackson], 8:310)

Charles's hymns, in particular, proclaim the limitless nature of God's love and grace. The mandate to share this good news is powerfully expressed in a little-known hymn (Osborn, *Poetical Works of John and Charles Wesley*, 5:126):

> *Teach me to cast my net aright,*
> *The gospel net of general grace,*
> *So shall I all to Thee invite,*
> *And draw them to their Lord's embrace,*
> *Within Thine arms of love include,*
> *And catch a willing multitude.*

Evangelism in the Wesleyan spirit is nothing less than wooing God's children back into God's loving embrace.

Evangelism, therefore, is the normal work of the whole church all the time. The Wesleyan understanding of evangelism as "gospelling" (proclaiming the good news) is powerfully expressed by Charles in this "Epistle" to his brother, published in 1744:

> *What then remains for us on earth to do,*
> *But labour on with Jesus in our view,*
> *Who bids us kindly for His patients care,*
> *Calls us the burden of His church to bear,*
> *To feed His flock, and nothing seek beside,*
> *And nothing know, but Jesus crucified?*
>
> *When first sent forth to minister the word,*
> *Say, did we preach ourselves, or Christ the Lord?*
> *Was it our aim disciples to collect,*
> *To raise a party, or to found a sect?*
> *No; but to spread the power of Jesus' name,*
> *Repair the walls of our Jerusalem*
> *Revive the piety of ancient days,*
> *And fill the earth with our Redeemer's praise.*

This hymn (Osborn, *Poetical Works of John and Charles Wesley*, 8:215) implies that evangelism is much more than preaching the gospel. The Wesleys clearly understood that Christianity is more caught than taught. As important as preaching was, therefore, of equal significance was the ministry of small groups within the Methodist structure. It would even be valid to claim that evangelism took place as much in the intimacy of the small group as in the anonymity of the crowd at major preaching events. Evangelism that is true to the Wesleyan vision must include a much larger process of evangelization. The elder brother emphasized this principle in a journal entry on August 25, 1763: "I was more convinced than ever that the preaching like an apostle, without joining together those that are awakened and training them up in the ways of God, is only begetting children for the murderer" (*Works*, Journal). The definitive organism of early Methodism, as we have seen, was the small-group meeting. In these circles, dedicated people learned what it meant to grow in Christ and together plumbed the depths of God's love for them all. But these cells also provided the foundation for the witness of loving service to others, an outward holiness that defined Methodist evangelism as well.

More than anything else, the early Methodists were convinced that love cannot be coerced. Nothing proclaimed Christ more fully than a winsome life. No methods of evangelism were employed, therefore, that were antithetical to its end. If love is the end, then love, and especially not fear, must be the means. Scaring someone into saving faith was a strategy the Wesleys would not countenance. And so John offered these suggestions in his *Advice to the People Called Methodists*:

> Above all, stand fast in obedient faith, faith in the God of pardoning mercy, in the God and Father of our Lord Jesus Christ, who hath loved *you*, and given himself for you. Ascribe to him all the good you find in yourself, all your peace, and joy, and love, all your power to do and suffer his will, through the Spirit of the living God. . . . Abhor every approach, in any kind or degree, to the spirit of *persecution*. If you cannot *reason* or *persuade* a man into the truth, never attempt to *force* him into it. If love will not compel him to come in, leave him to God. (*Works: Methodist Societies*, §22)

Several verses from John Wesley's translation of a German hymn, published first in 1738, strike the keynote of evangelism in the Wesleyan spirit. Here is a robust articulation of the gospel that takes pride in Christ alone:

> *The love of Christ doth me constrain*
> *To seek the wand'ring souls of men;*
> *With cries, entreaties, tears, to save,*
> *To snatch them from the gaping grave.*

> *My life, my blood I here present,*
> *If for thy truth they may be spent.*
> *Fulfil thy sovereign counsel, Lord!*
> *Thy will be done, thy name adored!* (Hymns [1780], 270)

In this hymn the movement from evangelism to mission is transparent. Unlike some forms of Christianity, the goal of which seems to be the redemption of one's own soul, the ultimate goal of Wesleyanism is the redemption of the other and the world. For this reason the Wesleyan tradition is implicitly missiological. Our charge is to glorify God, and we do so most fully by becoming the servants of all. The primary question for the Methodist is not, am I saved? The ultimate question is, for what purpose am I saved? For the Wesleys, the answer was clear. My neighbor is the goal of my redemption, just as the life, death and resurrection of Christ are oriented toward the salvation of all humanity. The self-giving love of Christ must therefore become the goal, purpose and style of our lives. The genuine Christian is the one who embraces the mission of Jesus in humility and servanthood.

Jesus lived his life in such a way as to proclaim that he came "not to be served but to serve" (Mark 10:45). His most dramatic sign of this servant mission was the washing of his disciples' feet on the eve of his crucifixion (Jn 13). His mission was characterized by healing the sick, liberating the oppressed and caring for the poor. In all of these actions he incarnated shalom, God's vision of peace, justice and well-being for all. If evangelism has to do with bringing people into the fold of God's love and care, then mission refers to the outward movement of God's people into places where lonely people dwell. Evangelism is the effort of the church to bring in; mission is the mandate to go out. Indeed, the word *mission* literally means "to go." The fundamental vision of Christian mission is being sent to continue and participate in the movement of God toward humanity that began with the mission, or sending, of Christ and the Holy Spirit. This is a mission of global proportions.

In his published journal, John Wesley transcribed a letter that contains one of his most famous statements: "I look upon *all the world as my parish*; thus far I mean, that in whatever part of it I am, I judge it meet, right, and my bounden duty, to declare unto all that are willing to hear the glad tidings of salvation. This is the work which I know God has called me to. And sure I am that his blessing attends it" (*Works*, Journal, June 11, 1739). The mission undertaken by the early Methodists was "to reform the nation, particularly the church, and to spread scriptural holiness over the land" ("Minutes of Several Conversations," in *Works* [Jackson], 8:299). In the opening pages of his *Advice to the People Called Methodists*, Wesley laid out the mission of his followers in this simple definition:

> If you walk by this rule, continually endeavouring to know, and love, and resemble, and obey the great God and Father of our Lord Jesus Christ, as the God of love, of pardoning mercy; if from this principle of loving, obedient faith, you carefully abstain from all evil, and labour, as you have opportunity, to do good to all men, friends and enemies; if, lastly, you unite together to encourage and help each other in thus working out your salvation, and for that end watch over one another in love—you are they whom I mean by Methodists. (§7)

Mission, on its most basic level, is nothing more nor less than offering Christ to others through concrete actions. While these deeds will be illustrated more fully in the next chapter as works of mercy, what remains for us here is to spell out the relationship between our words and our actions.

When mission and evangelism are separated, there is no substantive connection between Christ and the cultural context into which the Word is proclaimed. Those who champion this separation define evangelism solely as the proclamation of the good news, the goal of which is calling individuals into a saving relationship with Jesus Christ. On the other hand, there are those who believe that the purpose of mission is to facilitate social change, to make this world a better place. But Christian mission that flows from any source other than the good news of God's love in Jesus Christ is ultimately without substance and power. For some reason, many people have a hard time keeping mission and evangelism together without pitting personal salvation against social justice. The Wesleyan genius was to hold them together. Mission for the Wesleys was the effort to realize God's shalom in the world. Such a task is necessarily rooted in Christ, for we cannot speak of God's reign apart from Christ. The way in which the Wesleys envisaged this essential connection between evangelism and mission is one of their greatest contributions to the church today.

In her attempt to present an authentic Wesleyan perspective on the relationship between mission and evangelism, Dana Robert has made recourse to St. Paul's image of the church as a body (*Evangelism as the Heart of Mission*, pp. 3-5). In this paradigm there is an organic relationship between these two crucial ministries of the church; while evangelism is the heart, mission is the body itself. The body moves in different contexts, interacting, engaging, constantly at work. The dynamics of any setting determine in large measure how the body is called to respond. But the heart is always beating. It sends the life-giving blood throughout the whole. It nourishes the various organs and literally gives the body life. To separate the heart from the body is to kill it. Evangelism, the heart of mission, is to share the good news. But the body lives to continue the mission of Jesus in the world, namely to announce and demonstrate the reign of God. The heart and the body, evangelism and mission, Christ and culture, are interdependent and interconnected. This is the essence of the Wesleyan synthesis.

No example of this necessary connection is more compelling than the celebrated life of Mary Bosanquet. As a young convert to Methodism who had renounced the wealth and privilege of her early life, Mary committed herself to a plan of ministry and service. On March 24, 1763, Mary and her dear friend, Sarah Ryan, moved to Leytonstone in order to establish an orphanage and school. Wesley kept this model Christian community, which combined vibrant personal piety and active social service, under his personal surveillance. After much deliberation, the women determined to take in none but the most destitute and friendless. Over the course of five years, they sheltered and cared for thirty-five children and thirty-four adults.

Through their efforts, what might have become an elegant home became a school, an orphanage and a hospital—a center for evangelism and mission second to none. "We must not only preach the gospel, but live the gospel," one of the women in this circle argued, "or we shall do more harm than good" (Zechariah Taft, "Some Account of Elizabeth Dickinson," in William Bramwell, *A Short Account of the Life and Death of Ann Cutler*, p. 32).

These women provide an example well worth emulating. They incarnated in their own day an understanding of the Christian faith that was outgoing because it was centered in Christ. The Wesleyan vision of the church—the people of God—is one in which evangelism and mission are the essential activities of the whole people of God. While evangelism includes all of those activities that draw others in, mission reaches out to those who are most vulnerable and in need. In imitation of Christ we woo others into the loving embrace of God and then help them to see that their mission in life, in partnership with Christ, is to be the signposts of God's reign in this world. In his hymn "For a preacher of the gospel," Charles Wesley reminded us of this transforming call of God upon our lives:

> I would the precious time redeem
>   And longer live for this alone,
> To spend and to be spent for them
>   Who have not yet my Saviour known:
> Fully on these my mission prove,
> And only breathe to breathe thy love. (Hymns [1780], 421)

KEY TEXTS

BIBLICAL TEXTS

> It is too light a thing that you should be my servant
>   to raise up the tribes of Jacob
>   and to restore the survivors of Israel;
> I will give you as a light to the nations,
>   that my salvation may reach to the end of the earth. (Is 49:6)

I am the true vine, and my Father is the vinegrower. He removes every branch in me that bears no fruit. Every branch that bears fruit he prunes to make it bear more fruit. You have already been cleansed by the word that I have spoken to you. Abide in me as I abide in you. Just as the branch cannot bear fruit by itself unless it abides in the vine, neither can you unless you abide in me. I am the vine, you are the branches. Those who abide in me and I in them bear much fruit, because apart from me you can do nothing. (Jn 15:1-5)

JOHN WESLEY TEXT

If you walk by this rule, continually endeavouring to know, and love, and resemble, and obey the great God and Father of our Lord Jesus Christ, as the God of love, of pardoning mercy; if from this principle of loving, obedient faith, you carefully abstain from all evil, and labour, as you have opportunity, to do good to all men, friends and enemies; if, lastly, you unite together to encourage and help each other in thus working out your salvation, and for that end watch over one another in love—you are they whom I mean by Methodists. (*Advice to the People Called Methodists*, §7)

CHARLES WESLEY TEXT

A charge to keep I have,
 A God to glorify,
A never-dying soul to save,
 And fit it for the sky;
 To serve the present age,
 My calling to fulfil;
 O may it all my powers engage
 To do my Master's will.

Arm me with jealous care,
 As in thy sight to live;

And Oh! thy servant, Lord, prepare
  A strict account to give.
  Help me to watch and pray,
  And on thyself rely,
Assured, if I my trust betray,
  I shall for ever die. (Hymns [1780], 309)

FOR REFLECTION AND DISCUSSION

1. How do you shine your light for Christ in the world?

2. What kinds of fruit are you producing that point others in the direction of God?

3. Reflect upon the image of the vine and the branches. How is this paradigm for the church being lived out in your Christian community?

4. Is evangelism something you shrink from or are drawn to? Do you think of evangelism as something to which you are called or as a ministry for others? Why?

5. Describe a situation in which you witnessed Christian disciples engaged in mission that was totally selfless.

6. Reflect upon the image of evangelism as the heart and mission as the body. Is this a metaphor that makes sense to you? How has it changed your attitude toward both?

8

INCARNATIONAL MINISTRY
(SERVICE)
Piety and Mercy

Truly I tell you, just as you did it to one of the least of these
who are members of my family, you did it to me.

MATTHEW 25:40

In this final chapter we come full circle to the point where we began our journey. There is a close connection between faith and works, between the foundation of the Christian life and its fullness, namely a life characterized by acts of piety and mercy joined together in perfect love. In some ways, works of piety and works of mercy are nothing other than love of God and love of neighbor acted out in conformity to the love we see in Jesus Christ. Accordingly, to be perfected in the faith means to be as much like Christ as is possible in this life. There can be no doubt that this is God's greatest gift to us. For truly loving service springs from God's love in our lives. It is an answering love, a responsive love. But these are real actions in a real world. They are both personal and social. They are both spiritual and physical. The active life of love is characterized by a dynamic combination of worship and justice, devotion and compassion, spiritual resolve and social action. Holiness of both heart and life is the pattern of the believer who has become Christlike by means of God's grace.

We see the conjunction of works of piety and works of mercy most clearly in the life of Jesus. He was a man of prayer. He was devoted to the study of the Hebrew Scriptures, a rabbi who had immersed himself in the teachings of the Torah and the Prophets. His life was shaped by the Jewish festivals and feasts. No one could ever question that Jesus was a man of deep piety. But he also believed that his spirituality had to be lived out in a servant ministry to those around him. He clearly viewed himself as a suffering servant who was called to heal the sick, to feed the hungry, to release those who were in bondage and to proclaim God's reign to all.

Luke's account of the Transfiguration poignantly illustrates the conjunction of the spiritual and physical in the life of Jesus Christ. He and his closest companions ascended a mountain to pray. They were overwhelmed by the presence of God in a powerful spiritual experience. Despite Peter's pleading to remain there, apart from the world, to soak up this spiritual rapture, Jesus came down from the mountain with his disciples the next day. There Jesus was confronted by a boy who was writhing and contorted because he was possessed by a demon. This is exactly where Jesus was called to be in ministry (Lk 9:28-43). He intentionally immersed himself in the hurting places of humanity. He sought out those who were least and last and lost. He became what we are (as the great fathers and mothers of the early church would say) in order that we might become what he is. He took onto himself all the brokenness and fullness of life as we know it, with all of its joys and triumphs, with all of its pain and defeat. He lived out God's solidarity with us all.

Here is a parable of love itself. The loving person does not remain aloof from life. The loving person is not disengaged or protected from the brutal realities of this life. The loving disciple can never be uninterested in the plight of the poor, the weak and the broken. Rather, God's love reaches out to us wherever we are. The children of God who have been grasped by this love, like Jesus, invest themselves in the lives of broken and wounded people. People who are shaped by this kind of love are willing to get their hands dirty in the service of others in God's world, as Jesus did.

This essential discovery about the Christian life is nothing other than the "incarnational principle." For nowhere are the spiritual and the physical held together more closely than in the incarnation of God in Jesus Christ. The word *incarnation* literally means "to become flesh." And this is precisely what God-in-God's-love has done. In Jesus Christ, God entered into our physical world, in time and space, and became a human being, both affirming and redeeming all that we are. In a lyric paraphrase of Philippians 2:7, Charles Wesley said it well:

> He left his Father's throne above
> (So free, so infinite his grace!),
> Emptied himself of all but love,
> And bled for Adam's helpless race.
> 'Tis mercy all, immense and free,
> For, O my God, it found out me! (Hymns [1780], 193)

For the Wesleys, the implications of this central Christian truth were clear. The fact that God is Emmanuel (literally, God with us) means that the Christian is called to a life of incarnational ministry. It means that Jesus' disciples (those who learn how to love in his family) are also called to be apostles, those who are sent out as servants to incarnate that love for and with others. It is our task to make this spiritual reality (God's love) a concrete reality in people's lives. To be a Christian is to "flesh out" love. John Wesley drilled this point home repeatedly in his sermon "On Zeal," in which one passage explicitly affirms the synthesis:

> Are you better instructed than to put asunder what God has joined? Than to separate works of piety from works of mercy? Are you uniformly zealous of both? So far you walk acceptably to God: that is, if you continually bear in mind that God "searcheth the heart and reins"; that "He is a Spirit, and they that worship him, must worship him in spirit and in truth"; that consequently no outward works are acceptable to him unless they spring from *holy tempers*, without which no man can have a place in the kingdom of Christ and of God. (*Works*, Sermon 92, 3.10)

To be driven by a true Christian zeal means to combine holy tempers (a heart filled with love) with holy actions (open hands offered in loving service for others).

Charles captured such zeal in both the meter and the verse of a hymn written for his bride:

> *Come let us arise,*
> *And press to the skies;*
> *The summons obey,*
> *My friends, my beloved, and hasten away!*
> *The Master of all*
> *For our service doth call,*
> *And deigns to approve*
> *With smiles of acceptance our labour of love.*
>
> *His burden who bear,*
> *We alone can declare*
> *How easy his yoke;*
> *While to love and good works we each other provoke,*
> *By word and by deed,*
> *The bodies in need,*
> *The souls to relieve,*
> *And freely as Jesus hath given to give.* (Hymns [1780], 482)

Here is the secret of true happiness. Here is the joy of life given for others. Notice in the second stanza how "bodies in need" is connected with "souls to relieve." There can be no separation of the physical and the spiritual. And notice as well how both word and deed are required in order for the follower of Christ to give freely as the Master has given.

The Wesleys realized that works of piety devoid of compassion are pharisaical. They also knew that works of mercy not rooted in a grace-filled relationship with God are ultimately bankrupt. Acts of piety (which we have already explored at some length in chapters five and six), namely public worship, the ministry of the Word, the Lord's Supper, private prayer, searching the Scriptures and fasting or abstinence, when practiced in the right spirit, bring power and abundance to the Christian life. Works of mercy, which consist essentially of serving God and one's neighbor in the world, are the greatest source of our joy and blessedness. Both expand our capacity to love and our realization of true happiness in life. John made this abundantly clear in his sermon "The Important Question":

> It must also be allowed that as the love of God naturally leads to works of piety, so the love of our neighbour naturally leads all that feel it to works of mercy. It inclines us to feed the hungry; to clothe the naked; to visit them that are sick or in prison; to be as eyes to the blind and feet to the lame; an husband to the widow, a father to the fatherless. But can you suppose that the doing this will prevent or lessen your happiness? Yea, though you did so much as to be like a guardian angel to all that are round about you? On the contrary, it is an infallible truth that
>
>> All worldly joys are less
>> Than that one joy of doing kindnesses.
>
> A man of pleasure was asked some years ago, "Captain, what was the greatest pleasure you ever had?" After a little pause, he replied: "When we were upon our march in Ireland, in a very hot day, I called at a cabin on the road, and desired a little water. The woman brought me a cup of milk. I gave her a piece of silver; and the joy that poor creature expressed gave me the greatest pleasure I ever had in my life." Now, if the doing good gave so much pleasure to one who acted merely from natural generosity, how much more must it give to one who does it on a nobler principle, the joint love of God and his neighbour? It remains, that the doing all which religion requires will not lessen, but immensely increase, our happiness. (*Works*, Sermon 84, 3.5)

The Wesleys realized that the more one practices mercy and piety, the more mercy and piety begin to impinge on one another. But the primary insight of the brothers was that no act of worship or devotion is complete until God's love is carried into the world in concrete acts of compassion and justice.

John Wesley was never willing to leave any spiritual insight on a theoretical level. Spiritual principles had to be put into practice. Likewise, his spiritual direction was always clear, simple and realistic. His *General Rules of the United Societies* of 1743 are typical, revealing a simple and straightforward philosophy of life. First, do no harm and avoid every kind of evil. Second, do good and be merciful according to your power as far as is possible to all. Third, participate fully in the life of the church (*Works: Methodist Societies*, pp. 69-71, §4-6). Through twenty subsequent editions in his lifetime, these basic rules remained unchanged. Wesley's social ethic, which was essentially an ethic of love, can be summarized in this memorable statement, most likely the creation of a later Methodist imbued with the Wesleyan spirit:

> Do all the good you can,
> By all the means you can,
> In all the ways you can,
> In all the places you can,
> To all the people you can,
> As long as ever you can.

In the fourth installment of his preaching about the Sermon on the Mount, John indicated what this style of life would entail. "In order to enlarge your ability of doing good," he admonished, "renounce all superfluities. Cut off all unnecessary expense, in food, in furniture, in apparel. Be a good steward of every gift of God, even of these his lowest gifts. . . . In a word, be thou full of faith and love; do good; suffer evil" (*Works*, Sermon 24, 4.4).

Wesley practiced what he preached. Indeed, he had developed sensitivities in this area early in his life. In his sermon "On Dress," a sequel to his sermon "The Danger of Riches," he recalled a significant event from his school days:

Many years ago, when I was at Oxford, in a cold winter's day, a young maid (one of those we kept at school) called upon me. I said, "You seem half-starved. Have you nothing to cover you but that thin linen gown?" She said, "Sir, this is all I have!" I put my hand in my pocket; but found I had scarce any money left, having just paid away what I had. It immediately struck me, will thy Master say, "'Well done, good and faithful steward!' Thou hast adorned thy walls with the money which might have screened this poor creature from the cold!" O justice! O mercy! Are not these pictures the blood of this poor maid! See thy expensive apparel in the same light—thy gown, hat, headdress! . . . Be more merciful! More faithful to God and man! More abundantly "adorned (like men and women professing godliness) with good works." (*Works*, Sermon 88, §16)

He opened his eyes to the misery around him, and the social implications he drew from the gospel for his own day often have a disturbingly contemporary ring. In an effort to raise the consciousness of his contemporaries concerning the plight of the poor, he submitted the following editorial to *Lloyd's Evening Post*, entitled "Thoughts on the Present Scarcity of Provisions":

Why are thousands of people starving, perishing for want, in every part of the nation? The fact I know; I have seen it with my eyes, in every corner of the land. I have known those who could only afford to eat a little coarse food once every other day. I have known one in London (and one that a few years before had all the conveniences of life) picking up from a dunghill stinking sprats [small fish], and carrying them home for herself and her children.

I have known another gathering the bones which the dogs had left in the streets, and making broth of them, to prolong a wretched life! I have heard a third artlessly declare, "Indeed I was very faint, and so weak I could hardly walk, until my dog, finding nothing at home, went out, and brought in a good sort of bone, which I took out of his

mouth, and made a pure dinner!" Such is the case at this day of mul-
titudes of people, in a land flowing, as it were, with milk and honey!
abounding with all the necessaries, the conveniences, the superfluities of life! (*Works* [Jackson], 11:54, 1.1)

Toward the close of John's life, at eighty-one years of age, we find him
continuing the same legacy of advocacy for the poor. In the midst of the
harsh winter of 1784–1785 he "walked through the town and begged two
hundred pounds, in order to clothe them that wanted it most" (*Works*, Journal, January 4, 1785).

Certainly, a servant ministry entails the kind of self-sacrifice and self-
denial that John Wesley demonstrated in his own life. His followers both
heard and saw what an incarnational ministry would entail. His sermon
"On Self-Denial" revolves around the concept of the people of God engaged in a ministry that joins together evangelical piety and compassionate witness. He appealed to all lazy Christians who had lost their
first love and whose faith had become stagnant and lifeless. He diag-
nosed their spiritual ailment and prescribed the proper medicine that
would restore their appetite for the whole image and full enjoyment of
God:

He hath forgotten the word of God, "By works is faith made perfect"?
He does not use all diligence in working the works of God. He does
not "continue instant in prayer," private as well as public; in communicating, hearing, meditation, fasting, and religious conference. If he
does not wholly neglect some of these means, at least he does not use
them all, with his might. Or he is not zealous of works of charity, as
well as works of piety. He is not merciful after his power, with the full
ability which God giveth. He does not fervently serve the Lord by doing good to men, in every kind and in every degree he can, to their
souls as well as their bodies. And why does he not continue in prayer?
Because in times of dryness it is pain and grief unto him.

He does not continue in hearing at all opportunities, because sleep is sweet; or it is cold, or dark, or rainy. But why does he not continue in works of mercy?

Because he cannot feed the hungry, or clothe the naked, unless he retrench the expense of his own apparel, or use cheaper and less pleasing food. . . . Upon these and the like considerations he omits one or more, if not all, works of mercy and piety. Therefore his faith is not made perfect, neither can he grow in grace; namely, because he will not "deny himself, and take up his daily cross." (*Works*, Sermon 48, 2.6)

Central to his concern to hold acts of compassion and devotion together is the unmistakable teaching of Jesus on the sheep and the goats. "Truly I tell you," says Jesus, "just as you did it to one of the least of these who are members of my family, you did it to me" (Mt 25:40). Works of mercy that evolve out of the life of prayer will have a connection with the poor and will speak prophetically to the dangers of personal affluence—a blessing of God that is easily taken for granted. It should be no surprise, therefore, that the servant ministry of the early Methodist people was a mission lived out in solidarity with those people who were shut out, neglected and thrown away. Charles in his hymns and John in his preaching both admonished their followers to "make the poor their friends" (ST Kimbrough, *Songs for the Poor*). And they sang their way into the hearts and lives of these companions— those with whom they literally "shared their bread" (the actual meaning of the word *companion*):

> The poor as Jesus' bosom-friends,
>> the poor he makes his latest care,
> to all his followers commends,
>> and wills us on our hands to bear;
> the poor our dearest care we make,
>> and love them for our Savior's sake. (*ST Kimbrough*, Songs for the Poor, 3)

Or as they sang in one of Charles's greatest "Songs for the Poor" (recently rediscovered by ST Kimbrough):

Come, thou holy God and true!
Come, and my whole heart renew;
take me now, possess me whole,
form the Savior of my soul:
    In my heart thy name reveal,
stamp me with thy Spirit's seal,
change my nature into thine,
in me thy whole image shine:
    Happy soul, whose active love
emulates the Blessed above,
in thy every action seen,
sparkling from the soul within:
    Thou to every sufferer nigh,
hearest, not in vain, the cry
of widow in distress,
of the poor, the shelterless:
    Raiment thou to all that need,
to the hungry dealest bread,
to the sick givest relief,
soothest hapless prisoner's grief:
    Love, which willest all should live,
Love, which all to all would give,
Love, that over all prevails,
Love, that never, never fails.
Love immense, and unconfined,
Love to all of humankind. (ST Kimbrough, Songs for the Poor, 1)

The movement in this hymn is unmistakable. It is a movement from contemplation to action that connects evangelism and mission. It is a movement that holds together heart and hands. It is a movement that both puts worship at the center of a life of devotion to God and offers justice and mercy and compassion to all the children of God, whether they have found their way back to their true home or not. And notice in particular that it is "active love" that links our prayer to our service. A disciple with a living faith is the one whose whole heart has been renewed, who longs to radiate the whole image of God in his or her life and therefore hears the cry of the poor and wills, with God, that all should truly live! Here is a vision of the Christian life that unites piety and mercy, worship and compassion, prayer and justice. Here is a humble walk with the Lord that is lived out daily in kindness and justice. Here is an incarnational ministry that empties itself of all but love and finds its greatest reward in the realization of God's dream of shalom for all.

KEY TEXTS

Biblical Texts

Truly I tell you, just as you did it to one of the least of these who are members of my family, you did it to me. (Mt 25:40)

He has told you, O mortal, what is good;
   and what does the LORD require of you
but to do justice, and to love kindness,
   and to walk humbly with your God? (Mic 6:8)

John Wesley Text

Are you better instructed than to put asunder what God has joined? Than to separate works of piety from works of mercy? Are you uniformly zealous of both? So far you walk acceptably to God: that is, if you continually bear in mind that God "searcheth the heart and reins"; that "He is a Spirit, and they that worship him, must worship him in spirit and in truth"; that consequently no outward works are acceptable to him unless they spring from holy tempers, without which no man can have a place in the kingdom of Christ and of God. (*Works*, Sermon 92, "On Zeal," 3.10)

CHARLES WESLEY TEXT

> *Come let us arise,*
>> *And press to the skies;*
>> *The summons obey,*
> *My friends, my beloved, and hasten away!*
>> *The Master of all*
>> *For our service doth call,*
>> *And deigns to approve*
> *With smiles of acceptance our labour of love.*
>> *His burden who bear,*
>> *We alone can declare*
>> *How easy his yoke;*
> *While to love and good works we each other provoke,*
>> *By word and by deed,*
>> *The bodies in need,*
>> *The souls to relieve,*
> *And freely as Jesus hath given to give. (Hymns [1780], 482)*

FOR REFLECTION AND DISCUSSION

1. What might the characteristics of Micah 6:8 look like in our world today?

2. What acts of mercy and piety do you practice regularly?

3. How do we separate the physical and the spiritual in the church today?

4. Where do you feel God calling you into a ministry of service?

5. How would a life of committed Christian service change your lifestyle and your life today?

6. Reflect on the theological and personal insights that have captured you in this study. What next?

EPILOGUE

T he Wesleyan theological heritage is a tradition of living faith in which the purpose of theology is transformation. It is my hope and prayer that this study has provided an opportunity for you to grow in your faith and knowledge of Jesus Christ. I believe that the conjunctive theology of the Wesleys is an approach well worth emulating today. You have encountered eight different conjunctions related to the Christian faith in these pages. The challenge now is to put these lessons into practice. Faith working by love, leading to holiness of heart and life, is the key. This hymn by Charles Wesley says it well:

> Love divine, all loves excelling,
> Joy of heaven, to earth come down;
> Fix in us thy humble dwelling;
> All thy faithful mercies crown!
> Jesu, thou art all compassion,
> Pure, unbounded love thou art;
> Visit us with thy salvation!
> Enter every trembling heart.
>
> Finish then thy new creation;
> Pure and spotless let us be;
> Let us see thy great salvation
> Perfectly restored in thee;
> Changed from glory into glory,
> Till in heaven we take our place,
> Till we cast our crowns before thee,
> Lost in wonder, love, and praise. (Hymns [1780], 374)

Selected Bibliography

A. SELECT EDITIONS AND COMPENDS OF JOHN AND CHARLES
WESLEY'S WORKS

The Bicentennial Edition of the Works of John Wesley. Edited by Frank
Baker and Richard P. Heitzenrater. 35 vols. projected. Nashville: Abingdon,
1984–. (Volumes 7, 11, 25 and 26 originally appeared as the *Oxford Edition
of the Works of John Wesley.* Oxford: Clarendon, 1975–1983). Starred volumes are cited throughout the text.

*Vol. 1: *Sermons 1.* Edited by Albert C. Outler, 1984.
*Vol. 2: *Sermons 2.* Edited by Albert C. Outler, 1985.
*Vol. 3: *Sermons 3.* Edited by Albert C. Outler, 1986.
*Vol. 4: *Sermons 4.* Edited by Albert C. Outler, 1987.
*Vol. 7: *A Collection of Hymns for the Use of the People Called Methodists.* Edited
    by Franz Hildebrandt and Oliver Beckerlegge, 1983.
Vol. 9:*The Methodist Societies 1: History, Nature and Design.* Edited by Rupert E.
    Davies, 1989.
Vol. 11: *The Appeals to Men of Reason and Religion and Certain Related Open Let-
    ters.* Edited by Gerald R. Cragg, 1975.
*Vol. 18: *Journals and Diaries 1, 1735–1738.* Edited by W. Reginald Ward and Rich-
    ard P. Heitzenrater, 1988.
*Vol. 19: *Journals and Diaries 2, 1738–1743.* Edited by W. Reginald Ward and Rich-
    ard P. Heitzenrater, 1990.
*Vol. 20: *Journals and Diaries 3, 1743–1754.* Edited by W. Reginald Ward and Rich-
    ard P. Heitzenrater, 1991.

*Vol. 21: *Journals and Diaries 4, 1755–1765*. Edited by W. Reginald Ward and Richard P. Heitzenrater, 1992.

*Vol. 22: *Journals and Diaries 5, 1765–1775*. Edited by W. Reginald Ward and Richard P. Heitzenrater, 1993.

*Vol. 23: *Journals and Diaries 6, 1776–1786*. Edited by W. Reginald Ward and Richard P. Heitzenrater, 1995.

*Vol. 24: *Journals and Diaries 7, 1787–1791*. Edited by W. Reginald Ward and Richard P. Heitzenrater, 2003.

Vol. 25: *Letters 1*. Edited by Frank Baker, 1980.

Vol. 26: *Letters 2*. Edited by Frank Baker, 1982.

Charles Wesley: A Reader. Edited by John R. Tyson. New York: Oxford University Press, 1989.

John Wesley, *Explanatory Notes upon the New Testament.* 2 vols. 1755; reprint, Peabody, Mass.: Hendrickson, 1986.

John Wesley, *Explanatory Notes upon the Old Testament.* 3 vols. 1765; reprint, Salem, Ohio: Schmul, 1975.

Hymns on the Lord's Supper. In J. Ernest Rattenbury. *The Eucharistic Hymns of John and Charles Wesley*, 195–249. London: Epworth, 1948.

John and Charles Wesley: Selected Writings and Hymns. Edited by Frank Whaling. New York: Paulist Press, 1981.

John Wesley. Edited by Albert C. Outler. New York: Oxford University Press, 1964.

The Journal of Charles Wesley, M.A. Edited by Thomas Jackson. 2 vols. 1849; Kansas City, Mo.: Beacon Hill, 1980.

The Journal of the Rev. John Wesley, A. M. Edited by Nehemiah Curnock. 8 vols. London: Epworth, 1909–1916.

The Letters of the Rev. John Wesley, A. M. Edited by John Telford. 8 vols. London: Epworth, 1931.

John Wesley, *A Plain Account of Christian Perfection.* London: Epworth; Philadelphia: Trinity Press International, 1990.

The Poetical Works of John and Charles Wesley. Edited by George Osborn. 13 vols. London: Wesleyan Methodist Conference Office, 1868–1872.

Songs for the Poor: Hymns by Charles Wesley. Edited by ST Kimbrough Jr. New York: GBGM, 1993.

The Unpublished Poetry of Charles Wesley. Edited by ST Kimbrough Jr. and Oliver

A. Beckerlegge. 3 vols. Nashville: Kingswood, 1988–1992.

The Works of John Wesley. Edited by Thomas Jackson. 14 vols. 1872; reprint, Grand Rapids, Mich.: Baker, 1979.

B. ADDITIONAL WORKS CITED

Baker, Frank. *William Grimshaw, 1708-1763.* London: Epworth, 1963.

Beasley-Toplitte, Keith, ed. *The Upper Room Dictionary of Christian Spiritual Formation.* Nashville: Upper Room, 2003.

Church, Leslie F. *More About the Early Methodist People.* London: Epworth, 1949.

Crosby, Sarah. "Letter Book, 1760-74." In *Letters.* Perkins Library, Duke University.

Harper, Steve. *Devotional Life in the Wesleyan Tradition.* Nashville: Upper Room, 1983.

Jaeger, Werner W. *Paideia: The Ideals of Greek Culture: Archaic Greece and the Mind of Athens.* Translated by Gilbert Highet. 3 vols. Oxford: Oxford University Press, 1986.

The Methodist Hymn-Book. London: Methodist Publishing House, 1933.

Rattenbury, J. E. "The Methodist Prayer Book." In *The Methodist Recorder.* N.d.

Robert, Dana L. *Evangelism as the Heart of Mission.* Mission Evangelism Series, no. 1. New York: GBGM, 1997.

Snyder, Howard A. *The Radical Wesley and Patterns for Church Renewal.* Downers Grove, Ill.: InterVarsity Press, 1980.

Stromateis, VII, 10, 57. Quoted in J. Stevenson, ed., *A New Eusebius: Documents Illustrative of the History of the Church to* A.D. 337 (London: SPCK, 1957), pp. 199-200.

Taft, Zechariah. "Some Account of Elizabeth Dickinson." In William Bramwell, *A Short Account of the Life and Death of Ann Cutler* (York: John Hill, 1827), p. 32.

Thomas à Kempis. *The Imitation of Christ.* Edited by Harold C. Gardiner. New York: Doubleday, 1995. See Book IV.

Tooth, Mary. *A Letter to the Loving and Beloved People of the Parish of Madeley.* Shiffnal: A. Edmonds, n.d.

C. SUGGESTED FURTHER READING

Chilcote, Paul W. *Praying in the Wesleyan Spirit.* Nashville: Upper Room, 2001.

Chilcote, Paul W., ed. *The Wesleyan Tradition: A Paradigm for Renewal.* Nashville: Abingdon, 2002.

Clapper, Gregory S. *As If the Heart Mattered: A Wesleyan Spirituality.* Nashville: Upper Room, 1997.

Collins, Kenneth J. *John Wesley: A Theological Journey.* Nashville: Abingdon, 2003.

——. *The Scripture Way of Salvation: The Heart of John Wesley's Theology.* Nashville: Abingdon, 1997.

Harper, J. Steven. *Devotional Life in the Wesleyan Tradition.* Nashville: Upper Room, 1983.

——. *John Wesley's Message for Today.* Grand Rapids, Mich.: Zondervan, 1983.

Heitzenrater, Richard P. *The Elusive Mr. Wesley.* Rev. ed. Nashville: Abingdon, 2003.

——. *Wesley and the People Called Methodists.* Nashville: Abingdon, 1995.

Jennings, Theodore W., Jr. *Good News to the Poor.* Nashville: Abingdon, 1990.

Job, Rueben P. *A Wesleyan Spiritual Reader.* Nashville: Abingdon, 1997.

Kimbrough, ST, Jr., ed. *Charles Wesley: Poet and Theologian.* Nashville: Kingswood, 1991.

Knight, Henry H. *The Presence of God in the Christian Life: John Wesley and the Means of Grace.* Metuchen, N.J.: Scarecrow, 1992.

Langford, Thomas A. *Practical Divinity: Theology in the Wesleyan Tradition.* Nashville: Abingdon, 1983.

Maddox, Randy L. *Responsible Grace: John Wesley's Practical Theology.* Nashville: Abingdon, 1994.

Maddox, Randy L., ed. *Rethinking Wesley's Theology for Contemporary Methodism.* Nashville: Kingswood, 1998.

Manskar, Steven W. *A Perfect Love: Understanding John Wesley's "A Plain Account of Christian Perfection."* Nashville: Discipleship Resources, 2003.

Marquardt, Manfred. *John Wesley's Social Ethics: Praxis and Principles.* Trans. John E. Steely and W. Stephen Gunter. Nashville: Abingdon, 1992.

Matthaei, Sondra. *Making Disciples: Faith Formation in the Wesleyan Tradition.* Nashville: Abingdon, 2000.

Methodist Hymn-Book, The. London: Methodist Publishing House, 1933.

Outler, Albert C. *Theology in the Wesleyan Spirit.* Nashville: Discipleship Resources, 1975.

Rack, Henry D. *Reasonable Enthusiast.* Rev. ed. London: Epworth, 2003.

Runyon, Theodore. *The New Creation: John Wesley's Theology Today.* Nashville:

Abingdon, 1998.

Snyder, Howard A. *The Radical Wesley and Patterns for Church Renewal.* Downers Grove, Ill.: InterVarsity Press, 1980.

Staples, Rob L. *Outward Sign and Inward Grace: The Place of Sacraments in Wesleyan Spirituality.* Kansas City, Mo.: Beacon Hill, 1991.

Stone, Ronald H. *John Wesley's Life and Ethics.* Nashville: Abingdon, 2003.

Weems, Lovett H., Jr. *John Wesley's Message Today.* Nashville: Abingdon, 1998.

———. *Leadership in the Wesleyan Spirit.* Nashville: Abingdon, 1999.

Yrigoyen, Charles, Jr. *John Wesley: Holiness of Heart and Life.* Nashville: Abingdon, 1999.